PRACTICAL
ICE CARVING

PRACTICAL ICE CARVING

Joseph F. Durocher, Jr.

CBI Publishing Company, Inc.
51 Sleeper Street
Boston, Massachusetts 02210

Production Editor / Becky Handler
Cover Design / DeNee Reiton Skipper
Text Designer / Arabesque Composition
Compositor / Arabesque Composition

Library of Congress Cataloging in Publication Data

Durocher, Joseph F   1948-
     Practical ice carving.

     1.   Table setting and decoration.   2.   Ice carving.
I.   Title.
TX879.D87   642'.8   80-39990
ISBN 0-8436-2206-7

Printed in the United States of America

Printing (*last digit*): 9 8 7 6 5 4 3 2 1

CONTENTS

FOREWORD

Certain people in today's stressful world are methodically destroying the beauty of our environment. By contrast, entering a room where the ambience of a buffet is embellished and beautified by the ice carver's artful mind and skillful hands is a joyful experience.

The French consider the five great arts to be architecture, painting, sculpture, music, and cooking. For more than one hundred years, chefs and cooks have enhanced their buffet presentations with ice carvings, and occasionally with other culinary arts as well. These fine added touches provide enjoyment to the presentation of food and help people to relax.

Today's modern foodservices are dominated by fast foods and computer-assisted menu plans that often stress cost without considering aesthetic values or higher quality standards. Consequently, when our best resorts, restaurants, clubs, and hotels enrich fine food presentations with ice carvings, patrons will be reminded of that fine personal touch, so essential in all high quality foodservice.

Artful ice carvings are beautiful, and "a thing of beauty's a joy forever." These carvings add the same decorative touch to a buffet that flowers do to a table. They are often used to cool various foods or to display foods, as with "shrimp boats."

Ice carving is indeed a culinary art that must be preserved for high quality foodservice. Dr. Durocher's timely book on ice carving should help.

L. J. Minor, Ph.D.
Visiting Professor, HR & IM Department
    Michigan State University
Chief Executive Officer
    L. J. Minor Corporation, Cleveland, OH

PREFACE

Laboring over something with love, a bit of sweat, and—should it break—some tears can be depressing. If you have worked as most, your knuckles are sore, your feet are soaked as well as your clothes, and you wonder if it is worth it as you watch the puddle grow.

That pretty much sums up my first experience with ice carving. What a crazy idea to spend all that time and energy on something that would be reduced to slush on a hot day.

As a twentieth century artist (I use the term loosely), I knew that there must be a better way. That's where this book really began—in an effort to simplify the art form so it could be within the grasp of all.

I don't tell it all in this book... I don't know it all yet. Each time I start, some new technique comes to mind, one which may save time on the next carving or improve its appearance.

That doesn't mean the techniques might not work. I have taught ice carving to Navy and Air Force mess-management specialists who, as Ney-Hennessy Award winners, have participated in short courses at Cornell University since 1971. Hundreds of undergraduate and graduate students have also been exposed to, and have successfully participated in, this art form during special sessions I have offered at Cornell. The techniques have been refined to the point where they are nearly foolproof. Success will be nearly assured if you read before buying your first block.

I have learned from everyone I have taught. From Mike Ouimet and John Brominski, friends both of them, I have learned the most.

Enjoy and look for the next edition... I'm still learning.

J.F.D.

INTRODUCTION

In and of itself, ice is a humble substance; yet with some imagination, a few tools, and an understanding of the basic techniques presented in the following pages, nearly anyone can turn frozen water into a piece of art suitable to grace the center of an elegant buffet. Ice carvings have traditionally been created by persons with many years of practice, who often charge exorbitant fees for their creations. Although these fees may in some cases be justified, with only a little practice you too can confidently and competently create some of the more common forms of ice carving. In time, you will be capable of executing more elaborate carvings with professional expertise.

Getting started on your first ice carving can be very inexpensive. A six-point ice chipper, flat chisel, and large-toothed saw are the only tools you need to have before you buy your first block of ice. The ice will cost anywhere from $3.50 to $35 depending on your location and the availability of ice, and, with a total investment of less than $50, you can begin to carve your first creation.

ABOUT THE AUTHOR

A graduate of Columbia College, the author worked in the hospitality industry before returning to school at Cornell University, where he received the bachelor's, master's and Ph.D. degrees in hotel administration.

He taught in the School of Hotel Administration at Cornell while working on the Ph.D. and completing numerous and varied consulting projects for industry and government. Currently he is an associate professor at New York University teaching at the Center for the Study of Foodservice Management.

PRACTICAL
ICE CARVING

I
THE ART OF ICE CARVING

Although very intricate ice carvings require a great deal of artistic ability, the basic forms require only minimal skills. Following some fundamental techniques, including the use of a template, allows the beginner to create many carvings with ease. Previous experience in carving other media and in drawing are a help, but are by no means necessary for the novice ice carver.

Ice carvings have been used to adorn food displays for many years. We generally see ice carvings displayed only in the largest and most exclusive hotels in metropolitan areas, but their use is actually limited only by the availability of tools, supplies, and expertise needed to create the finished product. The photographs accompanying this book indicate the degree of intricacy that can be achieved in ice carving.

The Japanese are generally recognized as the masters of this art form, and they have provided us with some of the finest art pieces as well as carving equipment. Hideo Hasegawa is perhaps the most renowned practitioner of the art and has set forth his techniques in *Ice Carving*,* which is a pictorial compendium of his carvings. While his designs are excellent, they are unquestionably aimed at the Japanese market, and many would not be suitable for display in this country. The intricate carvings of Buddhist temples and Japanese teapots would not seem appropriate at a sports award banquet, for example.

Ice is beautiful by itself, and with the many facets an artist will carve into it, even the simplest forms can become dramatic attention-getting showpieces. Ice sculptures can be displayed by themselves or with other items to highlight presentations on buffets. They can stand alone as the alligator does, or be used to display flowers, the traditional application for an ice basket. The gondola is often used as the centerpiece for a cold seafood display with the space between the gunwales used to serve cocktail sauce. Lavished with food and flowers these pieces frequently stand out as the most memorable feature of a buffet.

*Hasegawa, Hideo, *Ice Carving,* (Palos Verdes, CA: Continental Publications, 1978).

ABOUT THIS BOOK

A kind of mystique currently surrounds the art of carving ice. Ice sculptures are held in awe not only by banquetgoers but also by many professional food-service operators who fear that esoteric skills are required for their creation. In fact, art works in ice can be produced by everyone, and it is the purpose of this book—through the suggestion of straightforward guidelines and the outlining of helpful hints—to bring this art form within everyone's reach.

II
CARVING TOOLS

The tools used in ice carving can be as expensive or inexpensive as the user wishes. There are, as mentioned earlier, three basic tools—chisel, chipper, and saw—which are essential for any ice carving. The following alphabetical list enumerates the tools that can be applied in ice carving, and incorporates recommendations for their possible purchase and various uses. Many of the tools are essential only to the artisan who wishes to hasten the carving process or to create more elaborate pieces. (See Figure 2.1.)

CALIPERS AND DIVIDERS

Calipers and dividers (Figure 2.2) are useful once the carving is taking shape. When carving the neck of a swan, the thickness of the neck as indicated on the template can be measured against the thickness being carved into the ice. Handles of pitchers and flower baskets can also be measured with these tools.

CHIPPERS

6-Point Chipper

The six-point chipper is a "must" for ice carving of all kinds. It is used when roughing out a figure, or when adding texture to the surface of such figures as the alligator or the hull of a ship. There are two types of chippers available in the market. Figure 2.3 shows a chipper fitted with hardened steel points set into a cast base. The chipper shown in Figure 2.3a has cast points as well as a cast base. As can be seen, the points of the hardened steel chipper are much sharper, and they can be sharpened further with a stone. The ice carver should not purchase a chipper with cast points. Not only can they not be sharpened, but the points bend and break off easily. Moreover, because they are not as sharp as hardened steel points, cast points make the chipper harder to use and require more pressure which could damage the carving in delicate areas.

1-Point Chipper

This tool is nothing more than an old-fashioned ice pick (Figure 2.4). You probably have one already. They are useful for chipping very small pieces, drilling out small holes, or scribing lines on the surface of the ice. If you purchase one, make sure that the handle is comfortable to hold. Some old chippers have large-headed handles which make them difficult to use when carving. Again, look for a hardened steel point which can be sharpened and does not break.

Figure 2.1. All you will ever need...and then some. (Courtesy of Visual Services/Office of University Relations, Cornell University.)

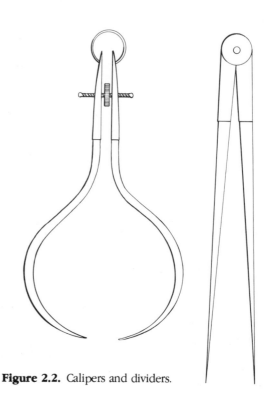

Figure 2.2. Calipers and dividers.

Figure 2.3. Hardened steel six-point chippers should be stored with a cardboard sheath to protect the points.

Figure 2.3a.

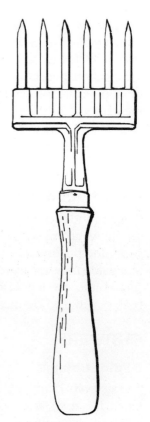

CHISELS

Angle Chisel

The angle chisel cuts a V-shaped groove in the ice (Figure 2.6). It is ideal for outlining a form on the face of the ice, for providing feathering on the wings of swans, and for grooves in the sides of bowls. Sizes range from ¼ inch on each side—useful for very fine feathering techniques—to 1 inch for less intricate work. These larger chisels are particularly helpful when outlining the shape of a carving on the face of the ice.

Flat Chisels

At least one flat chisel is a "must." A standard flat chisel used by a carpenter to carve wood will do quite

well (chisels used for cutting metal should not be used). You should choose one with a blade at least ½ inch wide. (See Figure 2.7.) Flat chisels used on a wood lathe are good for carving and are available in sizes up to 2 inches in width.

The narrow-tipped blade is good for scribing, chipping, and shaping in small areas. The wide blade is useful in obtaining smooth surfaces on large expanses of ice, for example, for smoothing the surface of a bowl once the shape has been roughed out. The better the quality of the chisel, the longer it will retain its edge. Both plastic and wood handles are available, and neither offers a decided advantage over the other.

Flat chisels made expressly for ice carving are more expensive than the conventional flat chisels available in your local hardware store. They are highly tempered, hold a good edge for a long time, and have handles designed specifically for the comfort of the carver.

Figure 2.4. Choose a 1-point chipper with a comfortable handle.

Figure 2.5. Chisels for the professional are available in complete sets.

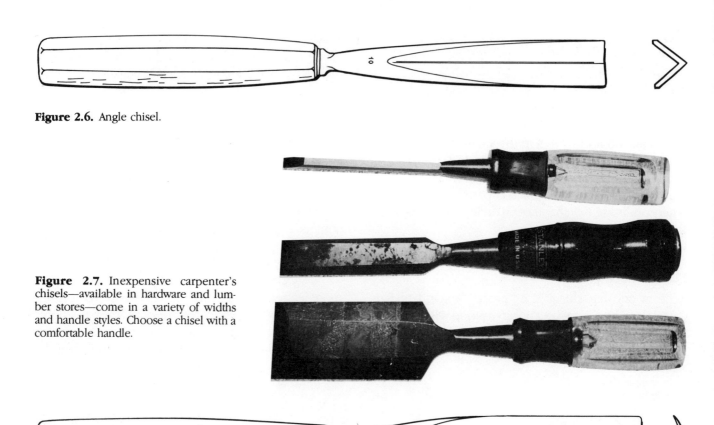

Figure 2.6. Angle chisel.

Figure 2.7. Inexpensive carpenter's chisels—available in hardware and lumber stores—come in a variety of widths and handle styles. Choose a chisel with a comfortable handle.

Figure 2.8. Round chisel (gouge).

Round Chisels (Gouges)

With tips shaped like a crescent moon, round chisels (Figure 2.8) are useful (although not necessary) when carving figures of living creatures, especially when properly shaping muscles. The rounded shape is also useful for grooving a display piece, such as the sides of a dish. For this application they are usually interchangeable with the angle chisel.

The sizes of available round chisels vary not only in distance across the face of the tip but also in depth, with some round-nosed chisels being closer to flat than other chisels.

Note: To facilitate the chipping and chiseling process, extensions to the handles of the chippers and chisels—made by attaching a cut-off broomstick or round hand rail—will increase your leverage and help protect your knuckles (Figure 2.9).

DRILL

While generally not necessary, hand-operated brace-type drills can be used for making or starting holes in ice. Electric, hand-held drills, fitted with straight drills or spade bits, are excellent for making holes to accommodate flower stems or to relieve pressure in the ice, as when carving out the canopy in a gondola, to prevent it from breaking.

Care must be taken not to force the drill, especially the spade bits. Forcing the drill will not significantly speed up the drilling process, and could lead to cracking the ice. If you use an electric drill, insure that it is double-insulated and grounded.

Figure 2.9. Chisels and chippers can be easily fitted with extension handles to facilitate their use.

MARKING PEN

A broad-tipped waterproof felt pen is ideal for sketching out templates (as discussed in a later section), and, if the ice is really cold, for tracing the shape of the template on the flat surface of the ice.

SAWS

Electric Chain Saw

While not necessary, an electric chain saw is useful to trim off large sections of the ice for final shaping. When making a cornucopia, for example, the saw can be used to quickly trim away excess ice from the backside, and to trim out the underside of the carving. It is also helpful in carving out the inside of the cornucopia from which the fruits of the horn of plenty will flow. The chain-operated saw offers one advantage over a hand saw: the nose can be pushed directly into the ice such as when carving out the pillars holding up the canopy of a gondola (Figure 2.10). In such cases, this tool can save the carver a great deal of time.

It is crucial that the saw be double-insulated, as with the drill, and connected to a grounded plug to prevent shock. Care must be taken to prevent injury when carving in a hot area because a great deal of water will cover the floor or ground and work tables.

The length of the blade is extremely important to consider. While ice is generally 10 inches (25 cm) thick, the prying teeth on some saws (used to aid in forcing the saw through a log) will hold a saw with a 10-inch blade away from the ice thus preventing the blade from cutting completely through the ice.

Another consideration is that, unlike gas-operated chain saws, electric chain saws operate at only one speed. This can be a distinct disadvantage at times. You must carry extension cords, and relying on an electric power source can be a restriction.

Gas Chain Saw

Used in much the same fashion as an electric saw, a gas saw can be used anywhere and does not entail the disadvantage of possible shock. It can be operated at slow or fast speeds, which is another advantage, but in closed spaces the exhaust fumes are a definite disadvantage. Also, the noise of the engine is worse than that generated by the electric saw. Finally, if you use a gas saw, you must carry around gas and oil for its operation, and, as with any internal combustion engine, starting it can be a problem.

Figure 2.10. Carving out pillars of a gondola.

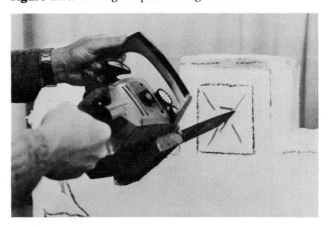

Note: Chain saw blades are lubricated with oil. It is essential that any oil be washed from the ice carving before it holds any foodstuffs for reasons of health and aesthetic appeal.

Hand Saw

Some kind of saw is essential, and hand saws are the cheapest. There are many types of hand saws with different lengths and types of teeth (Figure 2.11). Each one is best for certain uses, but generally a 12-inch to 24-inch large toothed saw is appropriate for most purposes. Some ice saws come with pistol grips, others with round handles, and still others with a handle similar to that of a wood-cutting saw (Figure 2.12). Each has advantages and disadvantages. The most important consideration in selecting a hand saw is the blade itself. The teeth must be large and have sufficient set to prevent binding. The better the quality of steel, the longer the teeth will remain sharp, and the longer the set will remain. Hand saws can be used for all functions performed by a chain saw except cutting pockets.

When properly used (when the saw is not forced), the hand saw places less stress on the ice than chain saws do. The cutting teeth of the chain saw are at least 1 inch apart and tend to cause vibration as they cut through the ice. This can often lead to the development of fractures. The beginner should use the hand saw and graduate to the chain saw only as the need arises.

SHARPENING STONE

Flat Stone

Keeping the chisels sharp not only saves time but also eliminates having to force the chisel on the ice, thus lessening the chances of the ice breaking or cracking. This stone can also be used for sharpening

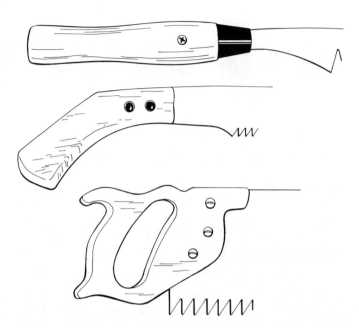

Figure 2.12. Sawhandle designs: choose the best for you.

the points of the chipper. An oilstone used for kitchen knives is perfect.

Round Stone

This stone can be used wet or dry and is only used for sharpening the round chisel.

SQUARE

When the carving process begins, a well-squared bottom is essential to safe handling of the ice. The large steel square (18 inches on one side and 24 inches on the other) can aid in squaring the bottom of the ice block before carving commences.

TONGS

If you plan to move the blocks around a great deal, tongs will greatly aid in this process. Borrowing them from your ice supplier, however, is cheaper and probably more feasible for the infrequent user than

Figure 2.11. Large-toothed, Japanese saws are excellent but expensive saws for ice carving. (Courtesy of J.B. Prince Co.)

Figure 2.13. Boston tongs generally require two-handed operation.

Figure 2.14. Compression tongs require only one hand once the tips are set in the ice.

Figure 2.15. A *surform* works nearly as well as a coarse rasp for smoothing ice.

buying them. There are two types; which to choose is a matter of individual preference. Boston tongs (Figure 2.13) are the simplest; compression tongs (Figure 2.14) are more costly yet allow a firmer grip on the ice block.

The Boston tongs are best used with two hands while the compression tongs—once set—can be used with one hand.

WOOD RASP OR SURFORM

A wood rasp is useful when imparting a smooth finish to the handles of a basket or other such form. Most of the work that a rasp will do is performed as a matter of course by the natural melting of the ice. The rasp is good to use for creating a smooth surface if the ice carving is going directly from the carving to the serving area for immediate display. (See Figure 2.15.)

YARDSTICK

The yardstick can be used to insure accurate adherence to the measurements of the template. It cannot be used in the same fashion as the calipers. For drawing straight lines a yardstick is superior to a tape measure, but if you already have a tape it will do. The yardstick is also helpful in setting up the grid pattern when making a template.

ADAPTING OTHER TOOLS FOR ICE CARVING

Most of these tools are not essential for the beginning ice carver, but many of the tools are probably in your possession already. It is worth noting again that the chipper, chisel, and saw are the only pieces absolutely necessary for the beginning ice carver.

Many of the tools I use for ice carving were intended for other uses. Once a very troublesome swan neck needed smoothing, but a fracture through the ice posed the danger of breaking the neck with any abrasive action. A blow torch used for browning meringue proved a highly unorthodox but handy tool in smoothing the neck. Use your imagination, and you will find that necessity is the mother of invention.

As you progress and are faced with new problems you too will find tools that can be used to solve special problems. Other pieces of equipment that can be used in ice carving will be explained in later sections dealing with specific carving techniques.

WHAT THE WELL-DRESSED CARVER WILL WEAR

There is no special dress required for ice carving, but understanding some of the options before you begin might save you a great deal of discomfort. Ice carving is not limited to any particular season and therefore your personal attire should match whatever is comfortable for you.

There are some pieces of attire in addition to your conventional clothing that are essential. Gloves are an absolute must. You will spend a great deal of time handling the ice and removing ice chips. Be it summer or winter, gloves make this process bearable. Some carvers use cotton gloves, but insulated, rubber-coated gloves are superior because they are waterproof and afford needed warmth when carving in the winter (Figure 2.16). Cotton gloves, when you are carving in a warm area, will soon become saturated with water and uncomfortable.

Gloves are also important because they protect your hands from the bruising effects of the ice. When chipping, your knuckles will frequently come into contact with the surface of the ice, and without the protection afforded by gloves, will get cut and bruised.

Preventing frostbitten fingers is another consideration. If you store the ice in a low-temperature meat freezer it will be held at temperatures near 0°F (−19°C). Handling the ice at this temperature, with no protective covering on the hands, can lead to frostbite.

Some sort of shoe covering is helpful, whether rubbers or boots. For most carvings you will be turn-

Figure 2.16. Rubber-coated gloves are superior to cloth gloves, as they keep your hands warm and dry.

ing about half of the block into little chips which melt quickly, and without foot covering, unprotected shoes become quite uncomfortable.

Some waterproof covering for the front of the torso is also helpful if you are using a chain saw. As the saw cuts through the ice it kicks a fine mist towards the operator. A disposable plastic apron of the kind used in many foodservice operations, or raincoat, will go a long way toward helping you stay dry.

As you chip the ice small pieces will fly off. Goggles will prevent these small chips from getting into your eyes. Although you can ease this problem by being very careful, wearing goggles makes the process just that much safer.

Having considered the equipment and attire needed for the first ice carving, let us now turn our attention to the medium itself: *ice.*

III
ALL ABOUT ICE

INTRODUCTION

Webster's defines ice in very simple terms, but it is actually a very complex substance. An introduction to the many sources of ice, guidelines on what to look for when carving ice, and an understanding of the basic structure of ice should all make the reader better prepared for ice carving.

Most of the carvings seen today are made from standard-sized blocks of ice measuring 10 inches × 20 inches × 40 inches (25 cm × 50 cm × 100 cm) each. A standard-sized block weighs in at nearly 300 pounds. There are times, however, when you may have to modify the size of the block by cutting it into pieces for smaller displays or by bonding several pieces together for a gargantuan display. Long before it is carved the ice must be *made,* and it is to that process that we now turn our attention.

SOURCES

Ice was first used in ancient India for the preservation of foods. The ice was sometimes manufactured through an evaporative process, and at times brought down from the Himalayas. The collection of ice in this country, from freshwater ponds and lakes, reached a peak in the early 1800s, at which time tall ships carried cargoes of ice all over the world.

NATURAL ICE

This kind of ice was taken from ponds, located for the most part in New England, insulated in thick blankets of sawdust, and stored for later use to refrigerate food in the summer. The process was laborious and required a good deal of risk, as has been documented in many newspaper accounts about horses falling through the ice during the "harvest."

The use of pond ice was limited by the difficulty of transporting the heavy blocks, storing them, and maintaining sanitary conditions in their production. Simply finding ponds with clear, sanitary water became more difficult near the end of the nineteenth century. When ice was taken from contaminated water, the bacteria held in the frozen ice were not killed but remained in a dormant state, later to multiply dangerously.

The quality of pond ice can be excellent for ice carving, but several problems limit its potential use. The pollution of ponds and lakes is greater today than it was during the past century, and finding a source of natural ice appropriate for use in food displays is more difficult than ever. Second, 10-inch-thick ice requires, with the use of a good saw, ten to fifteen minutes to cut from a pond, and only when it has been extracted from the water can you determine whether the ice is good for carving. When snow falls before the ice is frozen on top, subsequent rainfall will embed the snow in the ice block and render a very soft and opaque piece which breaks apart easily.

Harvesting ice can be an enjoyable project, and is an inexpensive source of ice for practice carving. If it has been allowed to develop without the incorporation of snow, under conditions of limited wind and reasonably constant temperatures, natural ice can offer excellent quality and clarity. The happy coincidence of all these optional conditions is rare, and therefore natural ice should not be relied on as a source for carving.

MANMADE ICE

The easier source, though more costly, is manufactured ice. The first manufactured ice was made in long sheets weighing up to seven tons. These sheets were frozen in large troughs and called *plate ice*. The long bars, as large as 10 feet × 20 feet × 1 foot, were cut into blocks.

The second technique, and the process most prevalent today, is *can ice* production. A distinct advantage of this technique is the ease of handling the blocks after they are frozen, each weighing approximately 300 pounds.

The cans, connected in groups of 36, are filled with water and then lowered into brine tanks. The brine tanks are filled with a calcium chloride solution of sufficient concentration to keep the brine from freezing at 15° F (−9° C), the temperature at which most can ice is frozen. The brine is chilled by expansion pipes which run through the brine tanks. Space between each of the cans allows the brine to circulate around the sides and bottom of the can.

The coolant most often used is ammonia which is compressed, and then draws heat out of the brine solution as it is allowed to enter the expansion pipes. A typical can ice plant turns out over 600 tons of ice each day, the equivalent of 7,200,000 Btu of cooling.

Figure 3.1. Over 10,000 pounds of ice are lifted at one time, decanted, and placed in storage at the Cape Pond Ice Company in Gloucester, MA.

Ice to be used for carving is processed in a similar manner to that used in producing regular can ice, with one difference: air is bubbled into the can of carving ice as the ice freezes. The purpose of this step is threefold: to equilibrate the temperature of the water as it freezes, to prevent the formation of large bubbles of air in the ice as it freezes, and to aid in the extraction of water impurities, thus rendering a clear piece of ice.

The water source is of greatest importance in making ice for carving. Most municipal water, although it has been treated, contains minute particles of dirt held in suspension. These particles react very similarly to sodium chloride particles in solution in seawater. As the water freezes, these particles are effectively squeezed from the water into small, highly concentrated pockets. (In salt water, this process leads to ice with a salinity content which is only 2 percent of unfrozen seawater.) The particles in the water are agitated by air pumped into the cans and are concentrated in the center of the can as the ice forms from the outer edges towards the center. Under normal conditions, the cans will freeze in twenty-four hours (slightly longer during warmer months and when the plant is at peak volume), and after twenty hours the cans are lifted from the brine. The water at the center of the now nearly frozen block, which has a high concentration of particles and is usually very dark in color, is decanted with the hole being refilled with fresh water. The cans are then returned to the brine and, without the aid of pumped-in air, allowed to freeze. Apparent in the center of carving ice is a cloudy core which is the water frozen without the clarifying assistance of pumped-in air.

The particles, suspended in the water, are squeezed from the ice as it forms into tightly bound hexagonal crystals. Because of this action, producing colored ice is difficult. If coloring is added to water before freezing, it reacts much like dirt particles suspended in impure water. Added to water, concentrated pockets of coloring occur as the ice freezes. This is particularly true if the water is agitated with air. Increasing the concentration of the coloring and not agitating the water helps effect an even dispersing of the coloring in the ice as it freezes.

Once removed from the cans, the carving ice must be handled carefully to prevent the development of fissures in the ice. The ice is generally frozen in a 15° F (-9° C) brine solution and then allowed to temper to 26° F (-3° C) in holding rooms. It is at 26° F (-3° C) that ice is most compact yet most pliable and least prone to cracking.

CAVEAT EMPTOR

Because ice has a tendency to become brittle as it ages it is best to carve ice close to the time it was made. Some people buy a number of blocks at once and hold them until needed, but this is an ill-advised practice unless delivery problems force you to purchase more than you immediately need. Not only does ice increase in brittleness the longer it is held, but there is a greater chance of it being struck and developing fissures which could later lead to breaks.

Temperature affects the quality of ice to a great extent. Fluctuations in the holding temperature of ice lead to weakening, especially when the temperature shifts between extremes, above 40° F (4° C) and below 10° F (-12° C). Fluctuations in temperature cause the ice to expand and contract which weakens the bonds in the ice and can lead to cracks.

Your supplier will give you some idea of the quality of the ice. If your supplier is also the producer of the ice, you are more likely to get ice of good quality than if you buy from a distributor who has to purchase the ice from a producer. Ask your supplier

where the ice comes from and at what temperature it is held. If it is stored below 15° F (-9° C), ask that it be moved to a tempering room (approximately 26° F (-3° C)) before being brought to you, especially during hot weather. This should not pose a problem because most suppliers have such a tempering room where workers bag ice and prepare it for shipment.

If your ice is discolored it is an indication that care was not taken in the freezing process. If the water is not decanted from the center of the block as it forms, and there are impurities in the water, the central core will be very nearly black. If the water poured back into the core is not pure, it too will lend a discolored appearance.

Excessive cloudiness is caused by air trapped in suspension as the ice freezes. This generally happens when the ice freezes without the agitation caused by air pumped into the ice. (Such ice is referred to as "mud ice.") The central core of carving ice is an example of cloudiness. If the bubbles are not large, the strength of the ice will not be affected. Cloudy ice is good for practice because it has all of the working qualities of carving ice but does not cost as much. Carving ice is generally more expensive than ice that has not had air pumped into it, sometimes four times as costly.

Air bubbles and soft spots are the direct result of poor procedures in freezing. If the ice is pulled from the brine tanks too soon and allowed to freeze in the storage rooms, air bubbles may become trapped in the center of the ice and weak spots may develop. Soft spots also result if the ice has not frozen completely. During the summer months, when ice production is at its peak, the ice may be pulled from the tanks before it is completely frozen; therefore, ice purchased in the summer should be checked carefully for weak spots.

Fractures in the ice are the biggest problem for the carver. Fractures will often lead to a break if not handled with care. Check the ice upon receipt for fractures. Keep the ice out of direct sunlight as just a few seconds in the sun can lead to the development of fractures. If your ice does develop a fracture it need not be discarded. Fractures running the length of the block preclude the carving of such items as swans, eagles, some numerals and letters, and baskets. Fractures running across the ice may preclude the carving of a horn of plenty or a swan, but will not prevent you from carving many figures where the block is situated in a horizontal position. If your ice has fractures, hold your template up against the ice to see how the fractures would affect the carving you plan. If a fracture goes only part way into the ice carving from one side of the ice you may produce perfectly satisfactory results, whereas carving from the other side might lead to disaster. It should be noted that fractures will often expand as pressure is placed on the ice whether from the shock of a chipper or the vibration of a saw.

Price is also an important consideration in purchasing ice. As mentioned earlier, cloudy ice is less expensive than clear ice and certainly appropriate for practice. If you will be carving figures smaller than a full-sized block, *scored ice* is less expensive even though it is still quite clear. This is ice scored by the producer to allow the distributor to divide the block into smaller pieces. In urban areas, there will also be significant price variances among suppliers. Another factor affecting the price of ice is the cost of delivery. *When getting a price quote, check not only the price of the ice, but also any delivery charges.*

With an understanding of the ice-making process and the qualities to look for in purchasing ice, you are better prepared to undertake the process of carving ice. Remember that ice is a very intricate and brittle structure. The freezing of water places extreme pressure on the water molecules as their actual form is changed to bring the molecules into an even hexagonal formation. While the ensuing bonding affords rigidity, it also leads to the brittle nature of the product.

IV

BETWEEN FREEZING AND CARVING

INTRODUCTION

Having gained some knowledge of the equipment and the ice used in ice carving, you are now prepared to investigate carving procedures and techniques—the subject of this chapter. There are still many steps to be performed before you chip into your first piece of ice. Understanding these steps and following them carefully will not only yield a better finished product but also greatly enhance your enjoyment of your newly found art form.

MAKING THE TEMPLATE

A *template* is simply a silhouette of the design you plan to carve into the ice. You will generally need only one template for each ice carving, most often a side view, but there will be cases in which it is appropriate to make a template for each end of the carving as well as a top view. Whatever you intend to carve, you will always need at least one template. The old adage "plan ahead" has never been more true than in ice carving. In many other creative endeavors, you can erase or cover up your mistakes. Once a piece of ice has been chipped away, the damage may well be irreparable.

It is important to begin with a design that is intricate enough to be interesting to the observer yet not so delicate that it will break easily. An ice carving of the Capitol building in Washington, D.C. would certainly be impressive, for example, but can be created only after extensive practice. The designs presented in this book are among the simplest, and are the designs most widely used in foodservice operations. But do not think that they represent a limit to what you can achieve.

The design you choose should complement the event at which the ice carving will be used. If you are presenting a buffet with a creole theme, the alligator can be displayed to add the feeling of a Louisiana bayou; if you need a centerpiece for your Thanksgiving buffet, the cornucopia is the ideal carving for the occasion.

There are many applications for special-interest designs as well. If you host Rotary Club luncheons and need a centerpiece to highlight the club's once-a-year evening banquet, you might consider carving the organization's symbol in ice. Other examples might be a wine goblet for a wine tasting, bells for a wedding, "GOOD LUCK" spelled out for graduates. Innumerable special-interest ice carvings can be designed to enhance presentations in a unique, personalized way.

PATTERNS FOR SUCCESS

The secret to creating any design is the template. Your first consideration in forming the template is the ultimate placement of the ice on display. If it is to grace the center of a buffet table 30 feet long, you should have no problems using a full piece of ice. If, however, you will be using the carving for an exclusive cocktail party, and the carving will sit on a 6-foot buffet table loaded with hors d'oeuvres, a carving from a half block might be more appropriate.

Once you have determined the size of carving you wish to create (and in most cases you will find that a whole block is appropriate), your next task is to make the template. Remember that the ice will in all probability measure 40 inches high, 20 inches wide, and 10 inches deep (100 cm × 50 cm × 25 cm) as it stands. Some producers might provide you with a block slightly larger or smaller than this standard size, and the measurement of the block should be checked before you make the template.

WHAT CAN YOU USE TO MAKE A TEMPLATE?

After selecting the design and the size of the carving, you must determine the type of material to use in making the template. Butcher's paper or wrapping paper can be used to make a single-use template. Paper is the cheapest material for a template, but it generally cannot be used again; during the process of tracing the outline on the ice, the template will freeze to the ice and usually tear as you try to remove it. Paper templates have the additional disadvantage of being difficult to hold against the ice during the tracing process, and they cannot be held against the ice once the carving begins.

If the design is one you intend to use again, you should probably select pressed wood (particle board), generally available in a 4 foot × 8 foot (1.2 meters × 2.4 meters) sheet. Templates made of this material will last for years if they are cared for, and have the advantage that they can be held up against the ice block as you carve. Once the design has been traced on the sheet of wood, a saw is needed to cut

the shape. (A paper template can be cut out with a pair of scissors or a sharp knife.) Care must be taken to keep these templates out of the water from the melting ice because, once soaked, they are prone to breaking. These 1/8-inch-thick templates are also easy to trace around. If you hold the chisel against the edge of the template, tracing the design on the ice can be as fast as tracing a line with a ruler edge; this ease is not possible with paper templates. Pressed wood templates take more storage space than their counterparts, but as a rule of thumb, if you intend to use the template at least once a year, you should make it from pressed wood.

MAKING THE TEMPLATE

Sketching the design can be accomplished by one of three methods: cross-hatch, overhead projection, or freehand.

To use the *cross-hatch* method, as depicted in Figure 4.1, draw a matrix with the lines forming squares across the face of the desired design. The squares of the matrix will allow you to create a more accurate copy of the design at the desired size than would generally be possible by drawing freehand. For example, the design being used in the accompanying illustration measures 3 inches × 8 inches (7.5 cm × 20 cm). To develop a template of a design this size, draw 1-inch square boxes across the face of the picture. Then, using the same procedure, draw squares on a 20 inch × 40 inch (50 cm × 100 cm) piece of paper with the lines 5 inches apart. For every inch

Figure 4.1. Cross-hatch method of drawing a template.

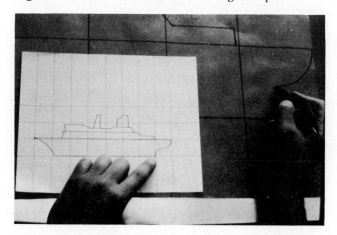

of length in the picture, allow 5 inches on the template. Because the ship is only 3 inches high, there are an extra 5 inches of the block not required for the ship. These extra inches can become the base which can be carved to represent waves, or can be cut from the ice block. For this example, the template will be drawn with 5 extra inches to be used as base.

The next step is to transform the small lines of the picture into lines on the enlarged template. Select one box through which the drawing runs. The stern of the ship is a good place to start. Note that the tip of the bow lies in the bottom of the left-hand center square of the picture. Find the matching square on the butcher paper and draw corresponding lines. Repeat this process for all the remaining lines on the outline of the ship. If the original picture includes lines indicating the deck level and other planes on the superstructure of the ship, these should be noted on the template. Once sketched, your design is ready to be cut out and become a template. If you are making a paper template and feel you might wish to use the design again, place the template on another sheet of paper and trace the outline. Put this second sheet away for a later carving. At a later date, if you find that you are using the template often, you can easily pull the design from storage and transfer the design for permanent use onto a piece of pressed wood.

The second technique is to use an *overhead projector* (Figure 4.2), which is somewhat more complicated than the cross-hatch approach. It requires equipment that, while not available to all, is generally available in most large hotels or through a rental service.

The drawing of the ship will be used again to explain this method. Special plastic sheets are available which, when fed through xerographic equipment in the same way paper would be, are imprinted with an image. The drawing of the boat is placed on the glass of the machine, the plastic sheet is placed in the paper tray, and with the push of a button your transparency is made. Tape a piece of butcher paper the size of the ice block onto the wall, place the transparency on the overhead, and focus the image to fill the entire piece of paper. You need only trace the image and cut it out of the paper and you have a complete template. Detail lines will not show up if the original drawing you have selected is a silhouette; however, if such lines are necessary, you might consider tracing them as you would have with the cross-hatch method. Producing extra copies of the templates is fast and easy. In many cases you may elect to make several different overhead transparencies at one time and then create the templates only as the need arises. As noted earlier, the templates will last indefinitely with proper care.

The third method is *freehand*, and if you have artistic abilities, this technique may well be the easiest. I suggest that you cut the paper to the size of a block of ice and begin sketching. Cut out the design and your template is ready.

It is important to remember, no matter which method you use, to leave a base on the ice. If you are

Figure 4.2. Using an overhead is easy if you have the equipment.

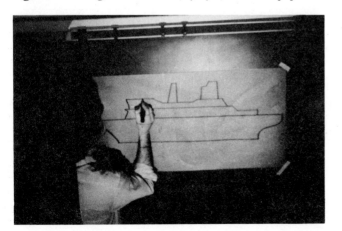

Figure 4.2a.

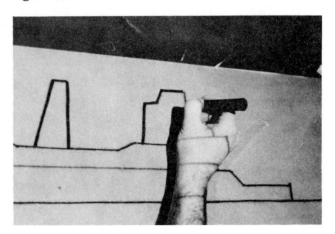

making a template of a ship, the base can be sculpted to resemble waves. In the case of a cornucopia or other upright carving, a substantial base must be left to prevent the carving from toppling over. The base need not be included as a part of the template, but, as in the case of an alligator on a pressed wood template, the addition of a base holds the alligator up in the middle of the block and thus allows for easier scribing of the figure on the ice. (It also prevents you from forgetting to include a base until it is too late.)

PREPARING THE ICE

If you need the ice carving for a particular occasion it is best to order the ice for delivery one day in advance of the function. The possibility of the ice breaking in transit and of other delivery problems is too great to take the chance of delivery on the day the carving is needed. If the ice appears to be extremely frosty, with what appears to be a fine snowy mist covering it, the ice has been held at temperatures below 15° F (-9° C), and should be tempered for best results. In such cases, place the block in a refrigerator for at least six hours before carving to allow the temperature of the block to rise to approximately 26° F (-3° C). The drip loss will not be significant because the block will not melt a great deal in such a short period of time. If, because of delivery problems, you must order the ice for delivery several days before you will be carving it, and therefore must store it in the freezer, set the ice on small blocks of wood that support the block at both ends and in the middle. If you fail to follow this precautionary procedure the block may become affixed to the freezer floor and be *very* difficult to release.

WHERE TO CARVE YOUR MASTERPIECE

When the time comes to carve the ice, you must find an area that you can reserve for at least two hours. Most carvings will take less than one hour to create but the extra time is needed for set-up and clean-up. Some carvers advocate carving in a refrigerator or freezer. I have never carved in one of these, and have no intention of doing so. Carving in a freezer does not permit the necessary tempering of the ice. Other drawbacks to carving in a freezer include:

1. It isn't very healthy; most of us do not keep a heavy winter coat available during July and, therefore, most carvers enter the freezer for an hour wearing street clothes and a chef's coat.
2. Cleaning up the numerous ice chips that will be generated in carving is a problem; any water that gets on the floor will quickly freeze and increase the chances of personal injury.
3. If yours is like most operations, you do not have a lot of extra space in your freezer. To hold a block may necessitate moving around some of your frozen foods. Moreover, it is next to impossible to move around freely in the freezer and carve with the interruptions that occur in an ongoing operation.

Carving in a refrigerator entails similar problems but generally not to the same degree. Personal health, disposal of the chips as they melt, and limiting access to the walk-in are the most obvious drawbacks.

No matter where you carve, you must insure that there is adequate drainage. There is nothing more dangerous than slippery footing when you are operating a chain saw. The drier the floor can be kept, the safer the process will be.

Carving outdoors—in a driveway, on the lawn, or on the loading dock—is an excellent choice (Figure 4.3). If you set a table on the lawn, remember that the block will weigh about 300 pounds. If the turf is soft, the weight of the block on the table may drive one or more of the legs of the table into the ground. Wherever the table is set up, it should be as level as possible.

Outdoor carving also has the advantage of easy disposal of the chips of ice and melting water. If you are using a gas-powered chain saw, an outdoor site is essential. Care must be taken when carving outdoors to keep the ice out of the sun. Melting caused by the heat of the sun is not the main problem in carving outdoors. Direct contact of the sun's rays with the ice may lead to the development of fissures. An audible crack accompanied by the development of a visible fissure in the ice can result from as little as ten seconds' exposure to the direct rays of the sun.

While carving outdoors is probably easiest, the location chosen should not be too far removed from the actual site of display. (I say this with some reserva-

Figure 4.3. Carving outdoors is easiest for ice removal but watch out for the sun cracking the ice.

tion, because one noted hotelier buys his carvings already completed by the ice men who make pieces to his specifications in the back of their delivery truck.)

MOVING THE MONSTER

Moving the ice can be laborious and possibly injurious if it is not accomplished with care. If you have tongs, make sure that the tips of the tongs are securely set in the ice before attempting to lift the block. Figure 4.4 shows the best placement for setting a pair of Boston tongs, how to hold them, and how to lift the ice.

Try to avoid setting either type of tong in the ice as seen in Figure 4.5, because lifting with the tongs in this position will place unnecessary strain on the

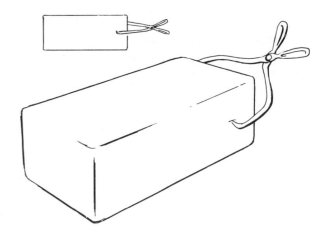

Figure 4.4. Boston tongs should be set in the ice near the end of the block.

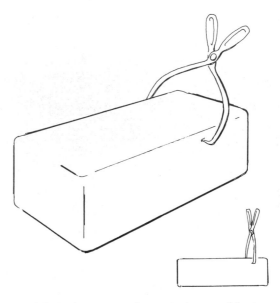

Figure 4.5. Setting any set of tongs in the top of the ice makes lifting the ice harder than it need be.

back. It is best that at least two persons work together in moving blocks of ice, with one person securing the tongs while the other steadies the ice as it is moved, thus preventing it from falling over.

A flatbed cart is the best means of moving ice. Low to the ground, thus facilitating moving the ice on and off the cart, this vehicle will not fall over because of its low center of gravity. When sliding a piece of ice onto a cart, one person should steady the cart to prevent it from rolling, another person should grasp the tongs, lifting the block onto the cart, and the third should assist in steadying and sliding the block onto the cart.

The most efficient and safest means of lifting a block from a cart to the carving or display table is the use of two tablecloth slings. A 90-inch or 72-inch tablecloth can be folded into a triangular shape (as seen in Figure 4.6) and then spun into a tightly twisted sling (Figure 4.7) which is tied tightly around the block, one on each end of the block. For maximum ease and safety, the aid of four persons, two on each side of the block, should be enlisted to lift the block.

When moving the finished carving, a similar process should be employed; be mindful, however, that the ice is more fragile after carving. For any carving, incorporate some form of lip under which the cloth sling can be secured. In lifting the swan (Figure 4.8), the sling is tied between the swan and its base, lifted by two persons, and steadied by a third. Never grasp a basket by its handles or a swan by its neck; the results should be obvious.

Check the carving table carefully before placing the ice on it. The ice will weigh 300 pounds, and if you stand on the table to do some of the work you should consider your weight in addition. Some banquet tables will just not withstand the weight and collapse, ruining the carving and perhaps the carver too. A cloth, a silencer, a thin piece of rubber, or some other covering should be placed on the table to prevent the ice from slipping.

READY, SET . . . GO

Squaring off the base of the ice block, whether the block is standing up or lying down, is the next step (Figure 4.9). The time required is well worth investing for both safety and aesthetic reasons.

Check with a steel square to see if what will become the bottom of the carving is square. Irregularities in the ice should be removed with either a chipper or saw. Recheck the block for square before beginning to carve. The need to square off the blocks also pertains to carvings incorporating more than one block. If two ends will be butted together it is especially important to square those ends to insure a correct bond.

Combining blocks of ice to produce a single carving is not advised for the beginner. The time will

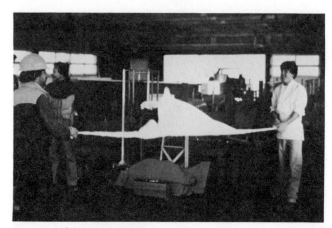

Figure 4.6. Sling triangle.

Figure 4.7. Tight sling.

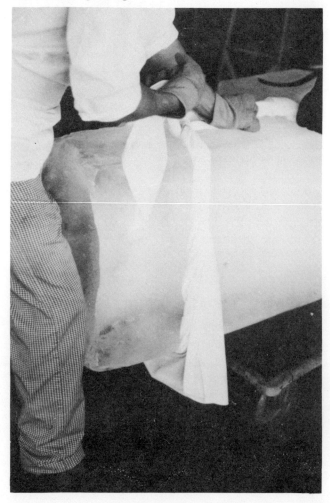

Figure 4.8. Use caution when lifting any carving.

Figure 4.9. Square the end of the block both vertically and horizontally; then cut with the saw or chipper before standing the block up.

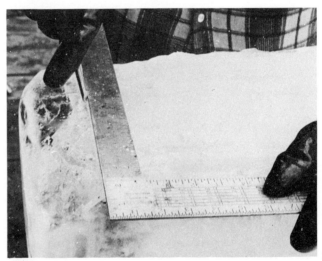

Figure 4.9a.

Figure 4.9b.

come, however, when you will be called upon to create a carving in which more than one block of ice is required. Not only do such creations weigh a great deal, but the time and manpower required to carve them is excessive. For the beginner, time is the most important concern as the ice will begin to melt and weaken if it is worked on too long.

A block of ice has an internal temperature of 15° F to 26° F (–9° C to –3° C). Moisture must be introduced between the surfaces of two blocks to be bound together. To accomplish this fusion, pour water on one of the edges, quickly press the two pieces together, then hope. The "cold sink" of the blocks draws heat from the water between the blocks, freezing it into a solid bonding agent. An alternative technique is to sprinkle the surfaces to be bonded with salt, not too much, but a dusting similar in amount to the dusting of flour on a baking sheet. The salt should not be the large, granular type; table salt works best. On some occasions the ice will not bind together, for example, if the blocks heat up enough that there is insufficient variance between their temperature and that of the water between them to freeze the water. In cases where the ice blocks do not freeze together, forming snow or ice chippings around the points where the ice joins may help. If you get really frustrated and must obtain a solid bond, either dry ice or your CO_2 fire extinguisher can lower the temperature of the ice enough to effect bonding. (Dry ice and CO_2 should be used only as a last resort.)

With the block securely set on the carving table, you are ready to scribe an outline of the desired carving on the ice (Figure 4.10). Position the template on the face of the ice (check for internal fissures in the ice to see that such fissures will not interfere with the carving) and, insuring that you have left space for a base, etch the outline of the template on the ice. The edge of the chisel tip, or a beer can opener, is best suited for etching the shape on the ice. Remove the template and go over the design, etching a groove ¼-inch to ½-inch deep wherever the etched marks were placed on the ice. The ice will only melt at about ¼ inch to ½ inch per hour and, because most carvings should be completed within this time, the outline should not have disappeared from the ice before you have completed the carving.

Figure 4.10. Scribing.

V

CARVING TECHNIQUES

Safety is the first consideration in ice carving. You are working with heavy, cold, bulky blocks of ice which, if not handled carefully, could cause severe bodily harm to you or anyone assisting you. Try to keep the floor as dry as possible. Be extremely cautious when using a chain saw and make sure when putting your saw through the ice that there is not an unwary hand on the other side. If you and another person are chipping on the same carving, watch where both pairs of hands are going. Do not use a gas-powered chain saw in an enclosed space. Be alert for frayed wires and other factors that can lead to shock when you use an electric saw or drill.

CARVE FROM THE TOP DOWN

If you carve the ice in any other way than from the top down, you might end up breaking off large pieces of the ice. As an example, when carving the cornucopia, remove the ice from the back side of the horn and begin to round off the back of the horn *before* you cut out the underside of the carving. Saws will help to remove large chunks of the ice without placing much stress on the ice. If a saw cannot be used, start shaping with the chipper.

ELIMINATE INTERNAL PRESSURES

When you eliminate internal pressures, you decrease the likelihood of the ice breaking. When carving out the handles of the basket, relieve the pressure in the ice by removing a section within the arch of the handles or by cutting an "X" in the center of the area between the handles; this will help prevent the handles from breaking later in the carving process. In carving the basket itself, after cutting an "X" through the ice, use the chipper to remove the ice, aiming as many strokes as possible toward the center of the block to minimize the stress on the areas through which the handles run. In smaller cut-outs, a drill can be used successfully to ease internal pressures.

FINAL SHAPING

You should perform the final shaping as close to the time that the piece will be displayed as possible. Bear in mind that particularly intricate pieces can break off in storage; putting the finishing touches on them is a step that can wait until just before service if the remainder of the piece is completed.

Remember that you are dealing with a substance that will begin to melt shortly after it is put on display.

Do not invest time in creating very intricate design work if the piece is to be used on a buffet because it may be removed from the freezer as much as two hours prior to service. All of your intricate work, work that not only takes valuable time but also, with every chip of the chisel, increases the risk of breaking the piece, might be sitting in the drip pan by the time your guests see the display. The melt rate varies, depending on the ambient temperature of the display area and the starting temperature of the ice, but averages ¼ inch to ½ inch per hour.

WORKING IN DETAIL

It is generally necessary to work in detail only when the carving will be used as a single service piece, that is, the carving will actually be presented to the guest as a serving vessel for one of the courses of the meal. In such cases, the detail should be worked in carefully, using tools that are as sharp as possible, and the ice should be well frozen. If the ice is close to the thaw state on the surface it will flake off in large pieces and ruin the display.

MELTING EFFECTS

Melting changes the structure of the ice as it sits during the carving process. If the ice remains in a warm location for too long (over 2 hours at 80° F (26.6° C) or above), the surface will begin to flake, much like flaked ice, and become nearly impossible to carve. Another melting problem arises when the piece is displayed. If you have carved a swan, bear in mind that the ice on top of the swan's head will melt and the resultant water will run down the beak and drop. This decreases the size of the beak as well as melting a gouge in the chest of the swan, and on some carvings this melting could ruin the appearance and possibly lead to breakage. Keep melting effects in mind as you plan your templates and ultimately carve your ice. For example, the four pillars that hold up the canopy of the gondola will always break near their bases where the greatest flow of melted ice water occurs, and it is therefore wise to keep the base of these pillars slightly heavier than the top.

USING THE THREE BASIC CARVING TOOLS

As mentioned earlier, there are three basic tools required for any ice carving. An understanding of the possible applications and correct use of each is essential to all ice carvers.

How to Use the Saw

Place the teeth of the saw on the line where the cut is required. Long, full strokes of the saw are the most effective and least damaging to the ice. *Do not force the saw.* If you find it is hard to move through the ice you have one of two problems, either the *set* on the teeth is not sufficient to prevent the saw from binding, or the teeth are inadequate to the task, being dull or too small. If you are using a hand saw that is not a real ice saw, with teeth suited to cutting finished lumber, the teeth will clog up with the ice-dust and slow the sawing process. For cutting very delicate areas, use a saw with smaller teeth as they will place less stress on the ice and be less likely to snag and break the ice.

Procedures for using the chain saw are similar to those for using the hand saw. Remember that you can control the speed of the gas-powered saw, but not the speed of the electric saw. Slower speeds should be used when you are using the saw in delicate areas for the final shaping. As mentioned earlier, the chain saw can be nosed into the ice, an advantage that hand saws do not offer. As a result, the chain saw can be used to cut pockets into the ice or to relieve pressures within the block.

How to Use the Chipper

To "rough out" the carving, hold the chipper as shown in Figures 5.1 and 5.2; this position affords maximum leverage and thus facilitates the quick removal of ice. (When holding the short-handled chipper in this fashion, gloves are essential.) For rough work, use a poking motion. Quick, short jerks of the hand, with the tips of the chipper lifting 4 to 6 inches off the ice's surface and striking the ice at an angle, are most effective for rough work.

Figure 5.3 shows the appropriate way to hold chippers when using them for more intricate work.

Figure 5.1. Holding the short-handled chipper.

Figure 5.2. Holding the long-handled chipper.

Figure 5.3. Chipper for intricate work.

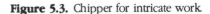

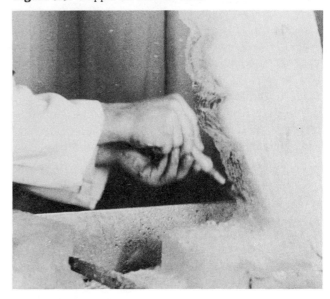

The tips of the chipper are set on the ice at a 30 degree angle, and the chipper is gently pushed across the ice. This technique produces fewer chips, is more controlled than the method above, and places less stress on the block of ice as it begins to take shape. Sharp points on the chipper are essential for finer work. If your chipper does not bite into the ice, either the angle of incidence between the chipper and ice is not great enough, or the chipper is dull.

How to Use the Chisel

Use short-handled and long-handled chisels much as you would the chippers. The chisel is most useful for smoothing surfaces and cutting grooves, and as such should be held as shown in Figure 5.4. There is no impact action, but holding the chisel at approximately a 30 degree angle to the surface of the ice, and sliding the chisel across the surface of the ice will achieve the best results. The chisel should be held

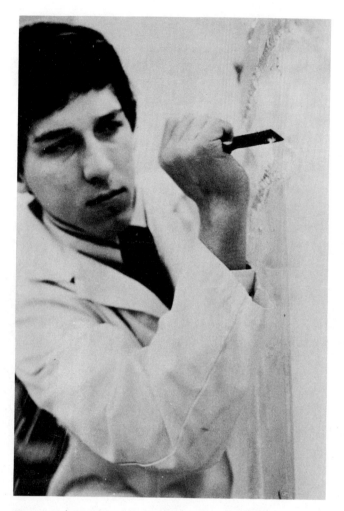

Figure 5.4. Holding the chisel.

Figure 5.5. The chisel should be held with the beveled side toward the ice.

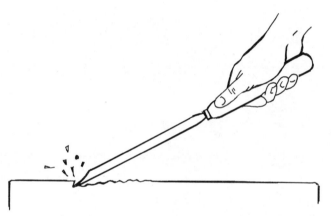

Figure 5.6. Holding the chisel with the flat side toward the ice will result in jerky action and make the ice chip away in rough pieces.

with the bevel side of the chisel towards the ice (Figure 5.5). Holding the chisel with the flat side to the ice will force it down into the ice, preventing a smooth gliding motion (Figure 5.6).

When using the chisel to put the finishing touches on a piece, carve *into* the piece as you smooth it rather than off the end of the piece. In smoothing down the pillars of the gondola, for example, the chiseling action should be from the canopy down toward the deck.

BUT WHAT IF IT BREAKS

The fear that every carver has need not be yours if you exercise caution. In the many carvings I have worked on, I have never broken the ice to the extent that it could not be repaired. Breakage can result from a blow, sitting in the sun too long, rushing to get the job done while not taking sufficient care, carving a piece to a dimension that is too small, and from moving the piece.

Salvaging the broken piece can be nearly as easy as breaking it in the first place if you use the same technique employed to meld two or more ice blocks together (as described in an earlier section). Suppose you have broken off the tip of the cornucopia. Simply fit the piece back on to the point at which it broke to see whether any pieces are missing. If the break was a clean one (and most are), coat one of the surfaces to be joined with salt and hold the piece back in place (Figure 5.7). If the ice is sufficiently cold, the bond will take place within two minutes. Make sure you wear gloves when you hold the ice in place, and don't move the ice once you have positioned it. If your first attempt fails, wash the salt off, resalt the broken piece, and try again. While holding the broken piece in place, have someone pack snow or ice chips around the break if you are having trouble effecting a bond. Such additional cooling will sometimes hasten the bonding process. Dry ice or CO_2 should be used only as a last resort. If all of these steps fail, and you must use the carving, a hole drilled through the broken piece into the solid part of the carving can be plugged with a dowel or a plastic rod to hold the piece together. Again, necessity will be the mother of invention.

STORING YOUR CREATION

If you must return the carving to the freezer before it goes on display, place small blocks of wood under the carving to prevent it from freezing to the floor. Remember, the ice is more fragile as a carving and should be placed where it will not be damaged. To protect the carving without interfering with food production, it may be wise to place the carving in a freezer remote from the location where it is to be displayed although moving the carving to the point of display may be less convenient for you.

Figure 5.7. If it breaks...

a. check broken piece

b. lightly salt broken face

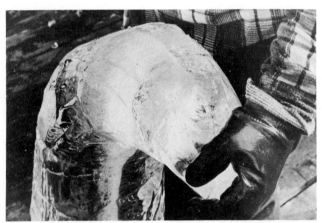

c. hold pieces together

d. et voilà

VI
CARVING BASIC ICE SCULPTURES

Remember that an ice carving is one of the most striking and memorable parts of a function; your guests will remember it long after they return home. Therefore, you want the carving to look as perfect as possible. To encourage this, you may try to work lavish detail into the carving, but remember that the detail may well be lost to melting before the guests see it, and that, with every strike of the chipper or chisel, you increase the likelihood of breaking the carving (perhaps irreparably). The novice carver, for example, may wish to make the neck of the swan *just* a little thinner, with predictable results. Keep in mind that your carving need only be *representative* of its subject; you are not making a real swan, boat, or alligator.

I was once asked to carve the Empire State Building for a charity function. Needless to say, because there is limited demand for carvings of this building, I had never tried it before. Carving the basic structure was a pretty straightforward task. A template outline was traced onto the ice, saw, chipper, and chisel worked away at the ice, and it began to take shape. I referred to a postcard photograph of the building as I carved and noted that the detail on the building was quite fine; very intricate work would be required to replicate all the features of the art-deco building.

Just as I began the involved task of etching in the many grooves of the side of the building, a five-year-old boy walking by exclaimed to his mother, "Look, Mommy, the Empire State Building." I packed up my tools and left. Take the example as good advice; pack up your tools before something goes wrong and resist the urge to make continual refinements. That last stroke well may well render all your earlier efforts useless.

STEP-BY-STEP PROCEDURES FOR CARVING A CORNUCOPIA (HORN OF PLENTY)

1. Check for fissures or cracks in the ice, and decide how to position the template on the block. Cracks running across the ice where the tip of the horn will be might pose problems.
2. Square off (10 inch × 20 inch on end) the bottom of block.
3. Stand block up and check for level.
4. Place the template on the block and scribe the outline on the ice (Figure 6.1).

Figure 6.1. Cornucopia (Step 4)

Figure 6.2. Cornucopia (Step 5)

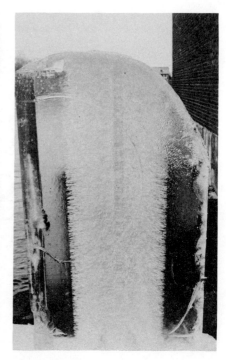

Figure 6.3. Cornucopia (Step 7)

Figure 6.4. Cornucopia (Step 10)

Figure 6.5. Cornucopia (Step 11)

Figure 6.5a.

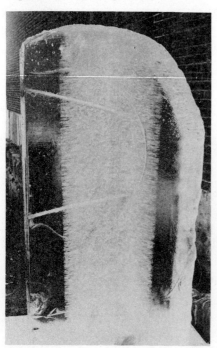

Figure 6.6. Cornucopia (Step 12)

Figure 6.7. Cornucopia (Step 13)

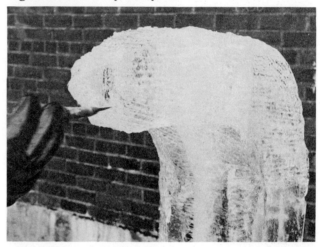

Figure 6.7a.

Figure 6.8. Cornucopia (Step 15)

5. Remove the template and chisel the outline in the ice approximately ¼ inch deep (Figure 6.2).

6. The scribing and chiseling process can be done on the reverse side of the block as well. (Take care when positioning the template on the reverse side to match its position on the first side.)

7. With your saw, cut a triangular piece to remove most of the ice on the back of the horn (Figure 6.3).

8. With the chipper, shape the backside of the horn to conform to the outline scribed onto the ice.

9. Round off the edges on the back of the horn with the chipper to approximately the middle of the horn as you look at it from the side.

10. With your saw make two cuts up to the line indicating the underside of the horn (Figure 6.4).

11. On a line running between the ends of the two cuts, chop straight into the ice with the chipper until the trapezoidal piece of ice loosens and falls out (Figure 6.5).

12. Round off the underside of the horn with the chipper (Figure 6.6).

13. Shape the top of the horn into a point by chipping into the ice (Figure 6.7).

14. Round out the lip of the horn with the chipper and chisel.

15. Chip in the underside of the horn where it meets the base by approximately 2 inches (Figure 6.8).

16. Smooth the surfaces of the horn with a wide chisel.

17. Carve out the mouth of the horn with the chipper and chisel. If you have a chain saw, nose the saw into the ice to expedite this step (Figure 6.9).

18. Tie a loop 6 inches in diameter in a piece of butcher's string 20 feet long.

19. Fit the loop over the tip of the horn (it should stop approximately 6 inches to 10 inches down the horn from the tip). See Figure 6.10.

20. Spiral the string down the horn until the base is reached. The string should spiral about 6 inches to 8 inches apart on each loop (Figure 6.11). When you reach the base, allow the string to hang loose.

Figure 6.9. Cornucopia (Step 17)

Figure 6.9a.

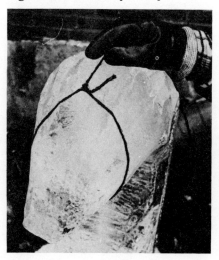

Figure 6.10. Cornucopia (Step 19)

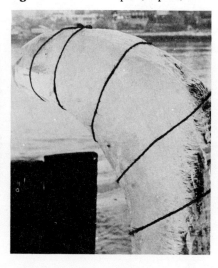

Figure 6.11. Cornucopia (Step 20)

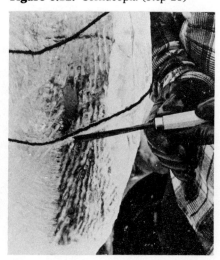

Figure 6.12. Cornucopia (Step 21)

21. With the chisel, etch along the lines where the string touches the horn (Figure 6.12).

22. Remove the string and carve a V-shaped groove where the string was using either an angle chisel or the flat chisel on either side of the groove. The groove should be cut approximately 1/2 inch to 3/4 inch into the ice and 1 inch wide (Figure 6.13).

For Display: Place carving in display pan and surround it with fresh fruits which flow from the mouth of the horn.

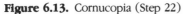

Figure 6.13. Cornucopia (Step 22)

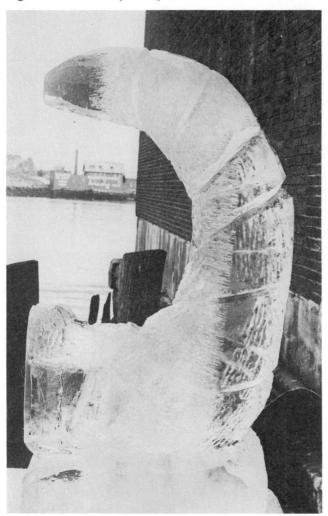

STEP-BY-STEP PROCEDURES FOR CARVING A FOUR-HANDLED BASKET

1. Check for fissures or cracks in the ice. In carving a basket, cracks that run across the block through the area where the handles will be carved could be particularly troublesome. Cracks in the base should not pose a problem unless they run completely through the ice.

2. Square off the bottom of the block (10 inches × 20 inches on end).

3. Stand block up and check for level.

4. Place the template on the block and scribe the outline on the ice (Figure 6.14).

5. Remove the template and chisel the outline into the ice approximately ¼ inch deep (Figure 6.15).

6. Remove the ice from the outer sides of what will be the handles of the basket. This can be accomplished most easily with the chipper. When sufficiently trimmed, the top of the handles will be semi-circular (Figure 6.16).

7. Trim the ice from the sides of the basket to form a shallow "V" on either side of the basket (Figure 6.17). This is most efficiently performed with a saw, but a chipper can also be used.

8. Round off the outside top edges of the handles with the chipper (Figure 6.18).

9. Remove the ice from the underside of the handles. This is one of the trickiest phases of the operation. *In making a hole through any piece of ice, hold your chipper at a 45 degree angle and always chip toward a center point* (Figure 6.19). Place an "X" in the center of the piece of ice to be removed and begin to chisel toward the center of the "X". When you have chipped halfway through the ice, repeat the process on the reverse side of the block. Once you break through there is less danger of cracking the ice. Continue to chip away at the ice until the underside of the handle is formed.

An alternate method is to cut an "X" through the part of the ice to be removed with a chain saw (Figure 6.20). Gently press the nose of the saw into the ice. (If someone is steadying the block for you, take care that they are not in the

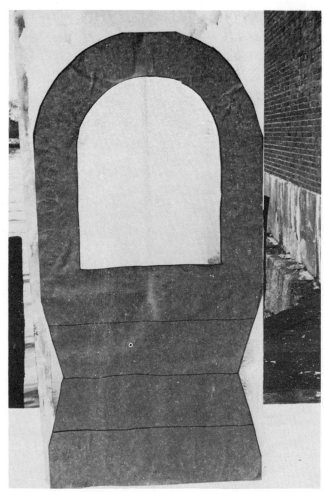

Figure 6.14. Basket (Step 4)

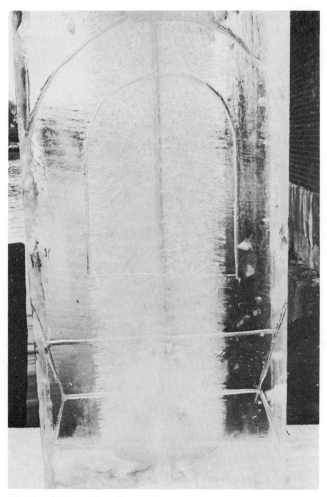

Figure 6.15. Basket (Step 5)

Figure 6.16. Basket (Step 6)

Figure 6.16a.

way when the blade exits on the backside of the block.) Remove the ice in the same manner as described above. Cutting an "X" into the ice lessens the internal pressures within the block as you chip away at it. If a horizontal crack develops in the ice during this process, all is not lost, but

extra caution should be used throughout the rest of the carving process.

10. Remove bullet-shaped sections of ice from the sides of the handles to give the appearance of four handles as follows: Looking at the block from the side, mark a point on the ice approxi-

Figure 6.17. Basket (Step 7)

Figure 6.17a.

Figure 6.18. Basket (Step 8)

Figure 6.19. Basket (Step 9)

Figure 6.19a.

Figure 6.20. Basket (Step 9)

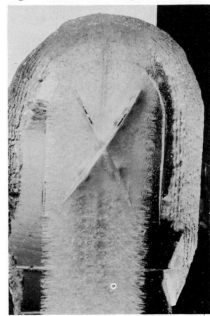

Figure 6.21. Basket (Step 10)

Figure 6.22. Basket (Step 10)

Figure 6.23. Basket (Step 10)

Figure 6.24. Basket (Step 11)

Figure 6.25. Basket (Step 12)

Figure 6.25a.

mately three-quarters of the way up the side of the handle (Figure 6.21). Place two marks on the ice, each 3 inches from the edge, where the handles connect with the base of the basket (Figure 6.22). Connect these two points with the third point to form what will become a bullet-shaped piece when removed. Repeat this marking process on the other side of the block.

With the chipper, begin to remove the ice, always chipping toward the center of the side of the block (Figure 6.23). Take care to limit the stress on the handles. An alternative method is to cut a slit in the ice with the chain saw and remove the rest of the ice, in much the same fashion as above with the chipper.

11. Round off the handles of the basket along the underside of the handles as well as along the cut-outs (Figure 6.24).

12. Looking straight down on the top of the block, mark a line across the top of the handles (Figure 6.25). With the chipper, chip a shallow "V" out of each side of the handles. This will further help the illusion of four handles.

13. Mark a line on the base of the basket connecting the "V" shapes cut in the sides of the basket.

Figure 6.27. Basket (Step 14)

Figure 6.26. Basket (Step 13)

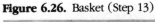

Figure 6.28. Basket (Step 15)

Figure 6.29. Basket (For Display)

Figure 6.29a.

Mark parallel lines 5 inches above and 5 inches below this line (Figure 6.26). With the chisel, carve a V-shaped groove at each of the three lines. It is very helpful to have a V-shaped chisel for this process, but a flat chisel will certainly work. Repeat this process on the reverse side of the basket.

14. Carve diamond shapes, intersecting with the horizontal lines above, with the points 4 inches apart (Figure 6.27).

15. The basket is usually used to display freshly cut flowers. A basin hole must be carved in the base to accommodate a frog to support the displayed flowers. When carving the hole with the chipper (Figure 6.28), take care to limit the pressure placed on the outside walls of the basket so as to prevent the side wall of the basin from breaking out. Leave walls at least 2 inches thick around the basin.

For Display: Spirals can be carved into the handles using a similar technique to that used with the horn of plenty (Figure 6.29). If the basket is to be used for a particular function, let's say a sales banquet for IBM, the initials of the company can be carved in relief on the face of the basket rather than the diamond shapes.

STEP-BY-STEP PROCEDURES FOR CARVING A SWAN

1. Check for fissures or cracks in the ice which would render it inappropriate for carving a swan. Because of the delicate nature of this carving, the ice should be as close to perfect as possible. A fissure across the ice where the neck will be carved spells almost certain disaster. The same is true for fissures running across the section of the ice from which the wings will be carved.

2. Square off the bottom of the block (10 inches × 20 inches on end).

3. Stand the block up and check for level.

4. Place the template on the block and scribe the outline on the ice (Figure 6.30).

5. Remove the template and chisel the outline in the ice approximately ¼ inch deep (Figure 6.31).

Figure 6.30a.

Figure 6.30. Swan (Step 4)

Figure 6.31. Swan (Step 5)

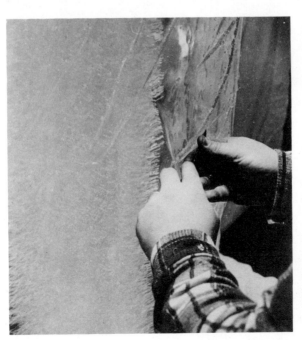

Figure 6.32. Swan (Step 6)

Figure 6.32a.

Figure 6.32b.

Figure 6.33. Swan (Step 7)

Figure 6.33a.

Figure 6.33b.

6. Remove the ice above the neck. This can be accomplished most effectively with the chipper (Figure 6.32). The ice should be trimmed down to the top point of the wing feathers.

7. Trim away the sides of the head and neck. The width of the head of the swan where the beak joins the head should be approximately 5 inches. The neck should taper back toward the body to a diameter of about 6 inches at the middle of the curve of the neck (Figure 6.33). Where the neck connects the body, it should be the full width of the body. An outside caliper is good for checking the diameter of the neck as it is tapered toward the body. As a rule of thumb, the neck should fatten gradually as it tapers toward the body.

8. Using the chipper, gently remove the ice from the underside of the neck of the swan nearest the head. Having removed the ice under the head, work toward the body.

9. Separate the wings from the neck by a single saw cut running parallel to the underside of the neck. Remove the ice on the underside of the neck with the chipper, and finish rounding off the neck (Figure 6.34). Note: If the neck is going to break, it will happen during this step so have a bucket of salt handy for quick mending. If the

neck does break, do not let it crash to the ground. Do not hang onto the neck as you work on the rest of the swan, and by all means make sure that everyone around the carving realizes you *don't pick a swan up by the neck.*

10. Shape the points of the wing feathers, and the points of the tail (Figure 6.35). This is best accomplished with a saw by cutting straight across the block along the lines of the template.

11. Separate the wings by removing the ice between them (Figure 6.36). Looking at the swan from the back, make two saw cuts which will form a long narrow "V."

Figure 6.34. Swan (Step 9)

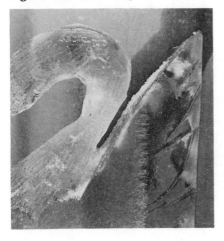

Figure 6.35. Swan (Step 10)

Figure 6.35a.

Figure 6.36. Swan (Step 11)

Figure 6.37. Swan (Step 12)

Figure 6.37a.

12. Feather the wings (Figure 6.37). To give the appearance of feathers the wings are formed with either the chipper or the chisel (the gouge gives the most realistic appearance).

13. Use the chipper to round out the body of the swan to the base working from front toward tail.

For Display: The swan is best displayed as a free-standing carving with bottom or back lighting (Figure 6.38).

STEP-BY-STEP PROCEDURES FOR CARVING A GONDOLA

1. Check for fissures or cracks in the ice which would render it inappropriate for carving a gondola. The ice will be set with the 10 inch × 40 inch side down. Any fissures running horizontally in the upper third of the block may prove troublesome when carving the bow, canopy supports, or stern of the gondola.

2. Square off the side of the block (10 inch × 40 inch side).

3. Lay the block down and check for level.

4. Place the template on the block and scribe the outline on the ice (Figure 6.39).

5. Remove the template and chisel the outline in the ice approximately ¼ inch deep.

6. Make saw cuts along lines A, B, C, and D. Using a chain saw is certainly easiest, but a hand saw will make these cuts perfectly well (Figure 6.40).

7. Remove the ice fore and aft of the canopy. With a chipper, strike straight into the ice along the deck line until the two large pieces are loosened (Figure 6.41). If your saw cuts have been made down to the deck line fewer than a half dozen strikes will be needed to remove each piece.

8. Shape the deck line. With the chipper, shape the deck line of the bow and stern.

9. Remove excess ice from the top of the canopy. With the saw, cut along the top line of the canopy (Figure 6.42).

Figure 6.38. Swan (For Display)

Figure 6.39. Gondola (Step 4)

Figure 6.40a. Gondola (Step 6)

Figure 6.40b.

Figure 6.40c.

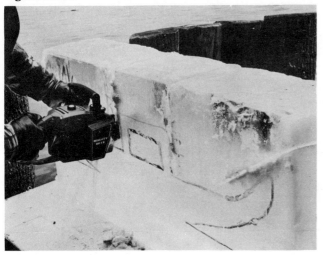

Figure 6.40d.

Figure 6.41. Gondola (Step 7)

Figure 6.41a.

10. With the chipper, remove the cut-out of the canopy. This step can also be accomplished with the chain saw by nosing the saw into the ice, then removing the remaining ice with the chipper (Figure 6.43).

11. Connect with the cut-out fore and aft of the canopy. A cut-out is made with the aid of a chain saw or the chipper on the fore and aft end of the canopy. Once completed, the roof of the canopy will be supported at each corner with a 2-inch square ice support (Figure 6.44).

Figure 6.42. Gondola (Step 9)

Figure 6.43. Gondola (Step 10)

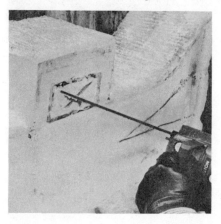

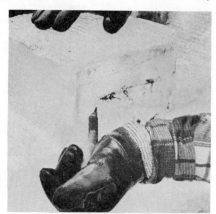

Figure 6.44. Gondola (Step 11)

Figure 6.44a.

Figure 6.45. Gondola (Step 12)

Figure 6.45a.

Figure 6.46. Gondola (Step 13)

Figure 6.46a.

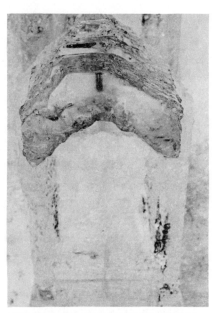

Figure 6.47. Gondola (Step 14)

12. Chip three wells into the deck. With the chipper and chisel carve a 3-inch deep well in the fore and aft decks and under the canopy leaving a 2-inch gunwale. These wells will be used later for displaying food (Figure 6.45).

13. Shape the underside of the bow. Two saw cuts can be made to remove the large triangular piece under the bow, or this process can be accomplished with the chipper. Use the chipper to shape the bow to a point from top to bottom. There are several notches in the top of the bow

which should be shaped with a narrow chisel (Figure 6.46).

14. Shape the underside of the stern (Figure 6.47). With the chipper, remove the excess ice from the underside of the stern and round off the stern slightly.

15. Shape the underside of the sides of the gondola with the chipper down to the water line. Leave the baseline (where the bottom of the boat intersects with the base of the block of ice) rough to resemble choppy water (Figure 6.48).

Figure 6.48. Gondola (Step 15)

For Display: The gondola is best displayed in a sea of crushed ice tinted with food coloring.

STEP-BY-STEP PROCEDURES FOR CARVING NUMERALS OR LETTERS

The procedures for carving letters or numerals are similar to those used for the aforementioned sculptures. The size and nature of the numerals or letters will affect the technique used in carving them. The following guidelines should be considered:

Size of Figures

For large displays, use one block of ice for each figure. Remember when doing this that a base is needed. For general display purposes, three figures can be carved from a single block of ice.

Relief versus Cut-out

The shape of the figure will affect how it should be carved. If you are carving "**IBM**" in one block of ice the following procedures apply:

1. Check for fissures in the ice.
2. Square off the side of the block (10 inch × 40 inch side).
3. Lay the block down and check for level.
4. Allow for a 4-inch thick base providing 16 inches height for the letters. Three inches of base should

be provided in front of the "**I**" and after the "**M**" as well as 3 inches between each of the letters.

There is sufficient strength in each of the letters that you can carve each letter through the entire block. If, however, you wish to create a centerpiece for a buffet for The Fighting "**449**"th you should carve the figures in relief onto the ice. The base of each of the numerals is so small, and the numerals are so top-heavy that should they be carved through the entire block, they might break away from the base. Therefore, it is best to scribe these numerals onto the ice and then carve out around the numerals approximately halfway into the block. Using this method, the chance that the numerals will break is significantly decreased.

This is not to say that all letters can be carved as a freestanding letter. The letter "F" would create the same problems as the numeral "4." A "4" or "F" could be carved as freestanding, but the chance of carving them successfully in relief is more probable.

WHAT ABOUT THE LEFTOVERS?

In a climate-controlled banquet room, your carving will melt at an average rate of ½ inch per hour. Of course, this rate will increase if light is directed on the carving, or if the room is extremely warm. As soon as the function is over, the carving should be returned to the freezer for storage and further use. If you leave a basket on display for three to three and a half hours, for example, you should be able to get a second use out of it. The same is true of most carvings, and some can be used three times. If, after the first use, some of the detail has melted away, return the carving to the freezer for at least six hours, then recarve the detail with your chisel. The carving is not ready to be destroyed even when the handles have melted away. The base measures approximately 16 inches × 16 inches, and if laid flat becomes an excellent bowl, with a little creative carving, for serving fruit salad, punch, or shrimp. A word of caution for those wishing to fill an ice bowl with punch: using dry ice—to give your punch that "bubble, bubble, toil and trouble" look—in a bowl carved out of ice will crack the bowl and allow your punch to leak away. Ice and dry ice do not mix.

VII
LET'S SHOW OFF A LITTLE

After a 300-pound block of ice has been chipped, chiseled, and sawed, the average carving will end up weighing approximately 150 pounds. Holding it safely for display in a public area is of serious concern, and must be considered even before the carving is begun.

WHAT TO HOLD IT IN

There are several containers designed specifically for holding carvings. Many of them are very elaborate devices suitable for the most elegant of dinner buffets. Others are made of high impact plastic (Figure 7.1). Homemade ones can be made very simply and relatively inexpensively out of galvanized sheet metal. The primary advantage to the galvanized holder is its alternative use as a cold bain marie for buffets.

The design of holders available commercially generally incorporates a holder, basin, and rack to set the carving on. The basin should have a drain hole with a spout to which a hose can be attached to draw off melting water. When purchasing one of these holders, check to see that they will accept the size of

ice carving that you intend to use most often. (Purchase information for these models is available in Appendix C.)

Although not nearly as elaborate, a homemade model can be fashioned at a local sheet-metal shop. I have found that a container measuring 5 inches deep × 30 inches wide × 72 inches long is the ideal size able to accommodate almost every carving. If you are displaying a stand-up basket, the basket can be surrounded in the pan with crushed ice and decorations; or bowls of cold food can be placed in the ice. If a gondola is to be set in the pan, it can be surrounded with an "ocean" of crushed ice colored with blue food coloring. Clams on the half shell, oysters, shrimp, and crab claws and legs can be lavished on the ice to provide a seafood bar your guests will not soon forget. As a point of reference, the galvanized container should cost no more than $50. Because it will be sitting flat on a table, it can be made out of 26-gauge sheet metal, with soldered joints and a rolled lip. While the purchased models are more elaborate, their cost and relatively delicate nature necessitate more care than the galvanized pan does. The pan—in and of itself, not very attractive—can be easily beautified by cloths draped around its edges.

Figure 7.1. High-impact plastic display pans are equipped with built-in drain pans.

MAKE IT A MEMORY

As mentioned in the previous section, an ice carving can be used as the focal point of a buffet table. Do not try to overdo the table with too many carvings. For one thing, the carvings are quite heavy and should too many of them be placed on a buffet table it might collapse. A second consideration is that the carving in most cases is designed to complement the food, not upstage it, or interfere with its presentation. If you are setting a 30-foot buffet with hot and cold food which will be freestanding—allowing guests to flow down either side—a single ice carving, placed just before the hot foods in the line, is most appropriate (see Figure 7.2). Do not place a carving at the very beginning of the line. It will not only obstruct the guests' view of food on the buffet, but, as your guests queue

up, it will be difficult for them to look at your carving carefully without blocking the line. Another advantage of using an ice carving (especially a tall one) is that guests can see where the cold food ends, and the hot food begins. There are times when a guest might wish to cut in for just one item on the line, and the carving can function as a "beacon" for finding that item. If you choose to have a second carving it might be appropriate to display it on another table holding desserts or beverages. If you have a double loaded buffet, with identical offerings on each end, the carving should be placed between the lines (see Figure 7.3).

When planning your buffet, consider the size of your carving in relation to the display area. If the carving is to be displayed at a cocktail reception where hors d'oeuvres are served, a carving of a gondola will probably be hidden by the throngs of people at the table. A low-profile carving is more appropriate for a buffet table where all guests will, by the nature of the service, see it while filing past the carving. Also, they should be able to view the carving from their seats once the lines at the buffet have dissipated.

A large carving can also be used at the entrance to a meeting room, or in the lobby of your hotel; two carvings could flank the front door. If you think a basket carved in ice and loaded with gladioli will grab your guests' attention on a buffet table, just imagine what it will do standing next to the lone doorman by the entranceway. If you are catering a function for **IBM**, the firm's logo carved in ice and placed at the entrance to the function room will unquestionably set the function apart from all others.

Individual carvings presented before each guest at a formal dining occasion are the epitome of elegant, personalized service. Such carvings can be

Figure 7.2. Two-sided buffet.

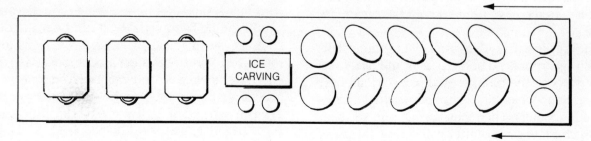

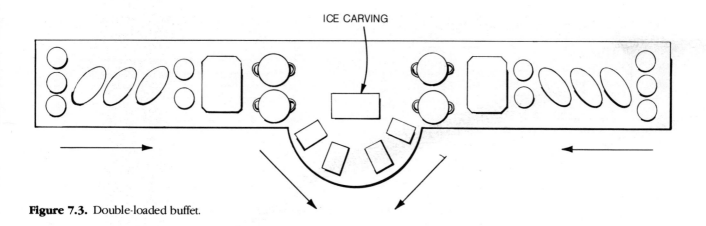

ICE CARVING

Figure 7.3. Double-loaded buffet.

decorative, functional, or both. For example, a sturgeon riding waves carved of ice with a tin of caviar nestled among the waves is not only decorative but very functional. Such pieces require extra care as the guests have opportunity to look at them closely for the length of the course. However, the labor required to prepare individual carvings may well pay off in publicity for your operation, and set you apart from most others.

LIGHTING: THE SECRET OF A JEWEL

Whether large or small, most carvings can be enhanced through the use of lighting, which highlights the carving's features. The lighting may be white or colored, depending on the nature of the carving, and the occasion for which it will be used. Ice reflects the color of the light beamed on it, and lighting can significantly improve the appearance of this humble substance. Facets and curves carved into the piece will pick up the light as a function of the relative positioning of the viewer, the ice, and the light source. Room lighting may negate some of the effects of special lighting.

If your carving will be viewed only from the front, back lighting is very effective. The light source should be, in the case of a flower basket or similar carving, placed behind the carving and aimed up at a 45 degree angle toward the center of the basket. This placement provides coloring throughout most of the basket without interfering with the guests' view of the piece.

Front lighting is often used incorrectly. The light might be hung from the ceiling and directed at the display. A glaring spotlight is not aesthetically pleasing and in the worst cases is placed far enough from the display that the viewer—getting too close to the carving—will actually cast a shadow thus negating the benefits of any lighting.

Can lighting is best when top lighting a carving and is also very effective if you have individual carvings on a dinner table. The light intensity can be high over the table prior to seating and subdued throughout the rest of the room with very striking effects. The light intensity should be lowered as the guests are seated at the table.

Another dramatic means of lighting a carving is from below. In the diagrams of the home-styled display rack (Figure 7.4) there is a light window in the base of the rack: the same is true of some plastic models. (See Figure 7.5.) A white fluorescent tube is the best light source. To obtain a colored effect, a gelatin (transparent colored sheets used in theatrical lighting) can be placed over the light window. One advantage of the fluorescent tube is that it produces little heat, compared with an incandescent bulb, and, because of its length, gives a more diffused light throughout the carving. If you do use bottom lighting, there must be a drain in the pan to draw off the water from the melting ice.

Remember when setting up any lighting to use caution to prevent electrical shock. Another caution in lighting is the type of bulb. A coated spotlight, with a tough-skin surface, is the best and safest to use. Don't make the mistake of using an infrared spotlight to give your carving a red hue as you will end up melting it more than lighting it.

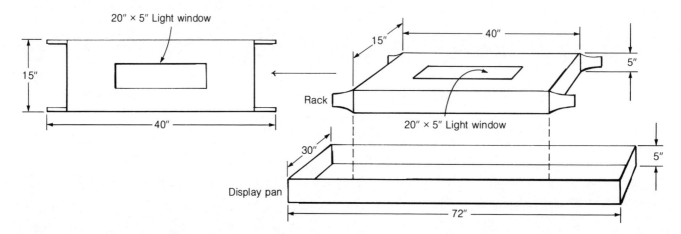

Figure 7.4. Homemade carving pan and display rack.

Figure 7.5. Plastic display bases that provide bottom light can afford your carving a dramatic touch.

Figure 7.6. A separatory funnel can be used to drip dye onto an ice carving to give colorful highlights to your masterpiece.

ANOTHER MEANS TO ADD COLOR

To provide for a highlight of color on your carving use a separatory funnel filled with the appropriate food coloring. The funnel is mounted above the carving, usually in a fishnet hung from the ceiling, and the coloring is allowed to drip slowly onto the carving (Figure 7.6). This highlight is especially appropriate for the neck of a swan, the head of a penguin, or the tip of a cornucopia.

PRICING FOR PROFIT

You can include the charge for the carving in the price of your buffet or charge for it separately. Depending on the size of the function, and the total charge in which the carving costs are included, I would advocate pricing the carving separately from the food and beverage charges.

Setting the price of the carving is your next problem. Remember all of the expenses incurred in preparing the carving—cost of ice, special carving or display equipment, set-up time for display, time to carve the piece—when calculating the price. A simple gondola of the type described in this book often sells for $150 or so. If you offer ice carvings on a continuous basis you will have all of the equipment, both

carving and display, and the only real costs new to each carving are those of the ice and labor. Assuming the ice costs $20, and the combined set-up time and carving time amount to about one hour, charging $150 may seem a bit out of line. If you can get that much money, more power to you, but remember there is more profit to an ice carving than the immediate swelling of the till. If more of your guests see your carvings—and more *will*, if the price is modest—your return will ultimately be greater because your customers will tell others about your operation.

VIII
ALTERNATIVES TO CARVING

If you are still not convinced that you can create your own ice sculptures, or if you are sometimes unable to expend the effort, you may elect to purchase ice molds. Fill them with water, stick them in the freezer, strip away the mold after the water freezes, and they are ready for display. It certainly is a lot easier, but you are limited to the molds available on the market.

The large molds (see Appendix A) can be used only once. They are filled from the top, frozen, and cut away from the sculpture with a sharp knife, never to be used again. Simple? Then why would anyone want to carve one? The limited variety of molds available, the cost of each mold (which far exceeds that of a block of ice), and the restrictions on creativity are but a few of the reasons for not using a mold. They take a long time—four to seven days—to freeze and, like the cheap can ice mentioned earlier, appear cloudy when frozen. Nonetheless, these molds do offer a real advantage in their convenience and ease, so if you are not up to the task of carving your own, look for them in your local restaurant supply house (or refer to the list of suppliers in Appendix C).

The small molds available on the market are quite different from the large ones in that they can be used over and over again (see Appendix B). These molds also offer greater flexibility because of the wider line of designs available. Once set in the freezer, they take approximately thirty hours to be completely frozen. They are ideal for single-service purposes or for use as focal pieces on cold buffet platters.

If you are really artistic, you can make your own reusable mold. Sculpt the form you wish in clay, and fire it as you would any other clay piece. Liquid neoprene and other rubber, available from numerous suppliers, can be poured around your form and allowed to set. Carefully cut the rubber away, remove the form, and you have a mold you can use over and over again. Drill a hole through which water can be added, press the parts of the mold back together again, holding them together with a clamp, and you are ready to make your own customized carvings.

ONCE AGAIN

Ice carving is ideal for almost everyone. With minimal effort on your part you can create beautiful and functional pieces to enhance your operation. If you follow these simple procedures success is virtually guaranteed. Happy chipping!

APPENDIX A
Large Ice Molds

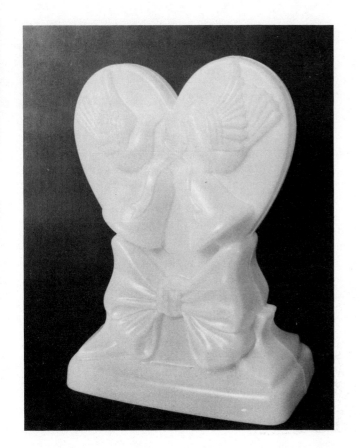

Photos courtesy of J. B. Prince Company.

APPENDIX B
Small, Reusable
Ice Molds

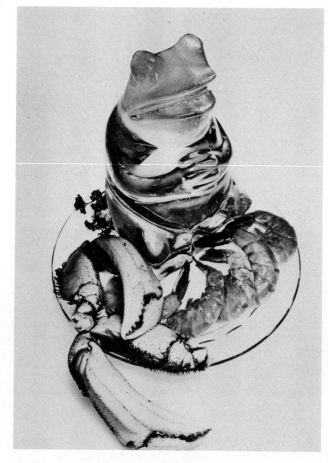

SMALL DOLPHIN
8″ high

PENGUIN
9½″ high

FROG
6″ high

TREE
7″ high

BUNNY
9″ high

TEDDY BEAR
8½″ high

CASTLE
8½″ high

DUCK
8½" high

POLAR BEAR
8½" high

FISH
8½" high

SWAN
8½" high

LARGE DOLPHIN
8½″ high

TURKEY
8½″ high

SEAL
7½″ high

ARTICHOKE
7½″ high

Photos courtesy of CBL Specialties Inc., San Leandro, CA.

APPENDIX C
Suppliers

J.B. Prince Company
236 Berkeley Place
Brooklyn, NY 11217
(212) 638-3737

    The J.B. Prince Company is a nationwide mail order source for professional chef's tools, utensils, and equipment. They have nearly everything needed for working in ice or displaying it, even large molds if you don't wish to carve your own.

CBL Specialties, Inc.
P.O. Box 644
San Leandro, CA 94577
(415) 357-3039

    CBL Specialties, Inc. is the manufacturer of the reusable molds pictured in the appendix. The molds are available in restaurant supply and specialty stores. Should you be unable to find their products, they may be contacted directly.

Pro Chef International, Inc.
900 Silver Spur Road
P.O. Box 2218
Palos Verdes, CA 90274

    Pro Chef International, Inc. manufactures carving tools and display stands for ice carvings.

APPENDIX D
Templates

The grid squares on the following
pages are equivalent to
5 inches on a full size template

CORNUCOPIA

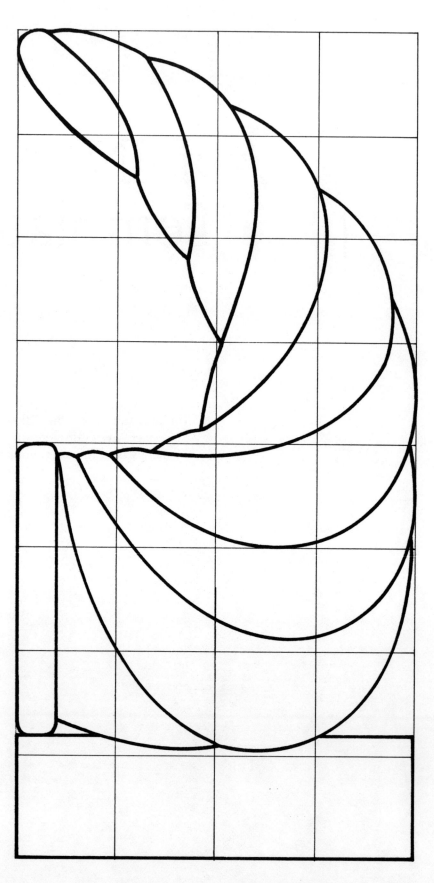

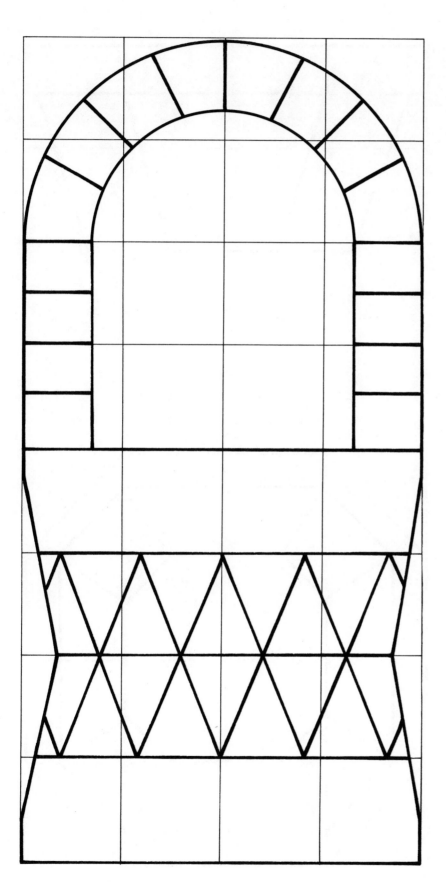

BASKET

BOWL (½ block)

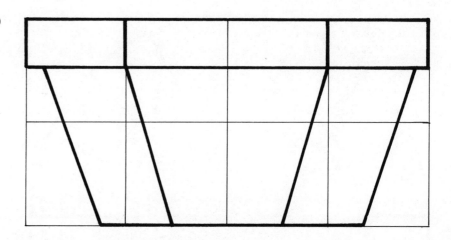

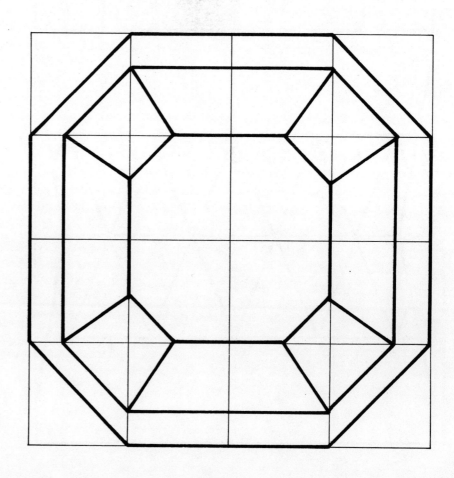

SWAN

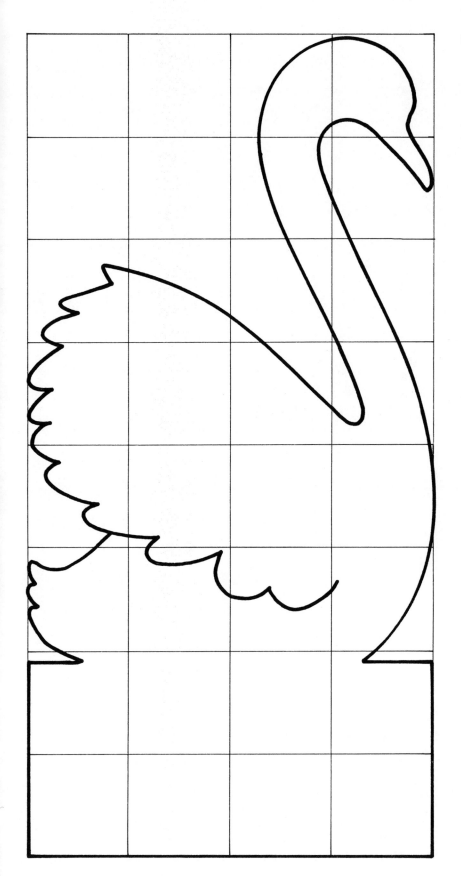

EAGLE

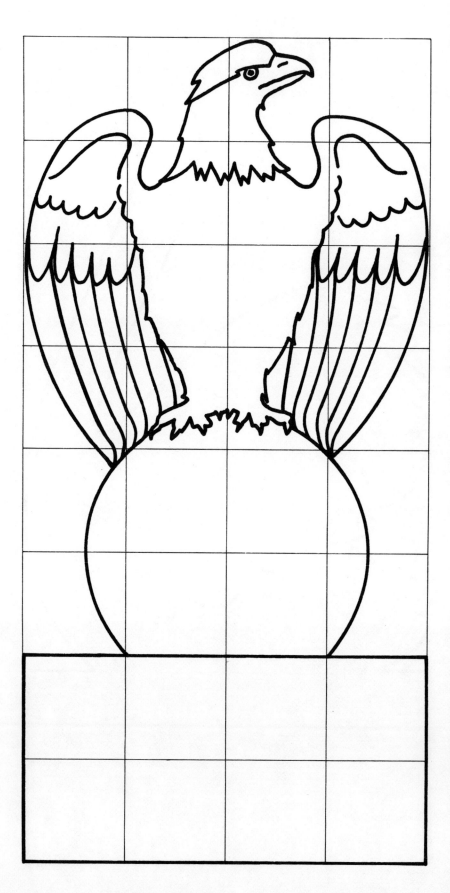

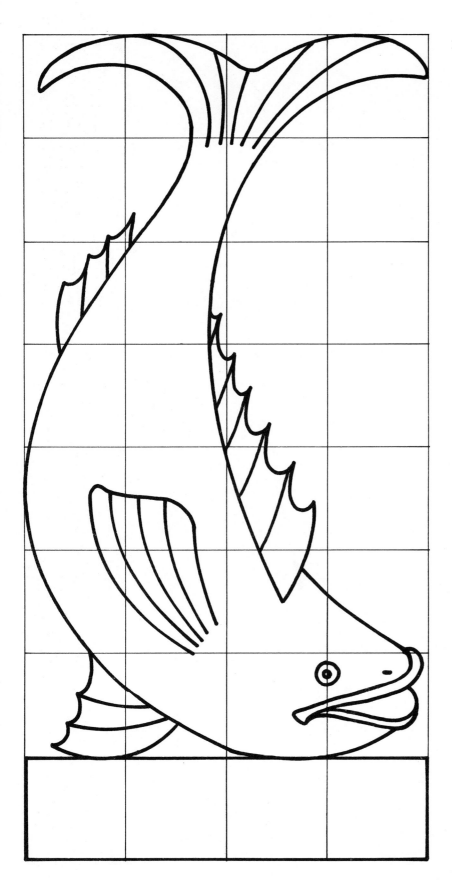

FISH

SEAL

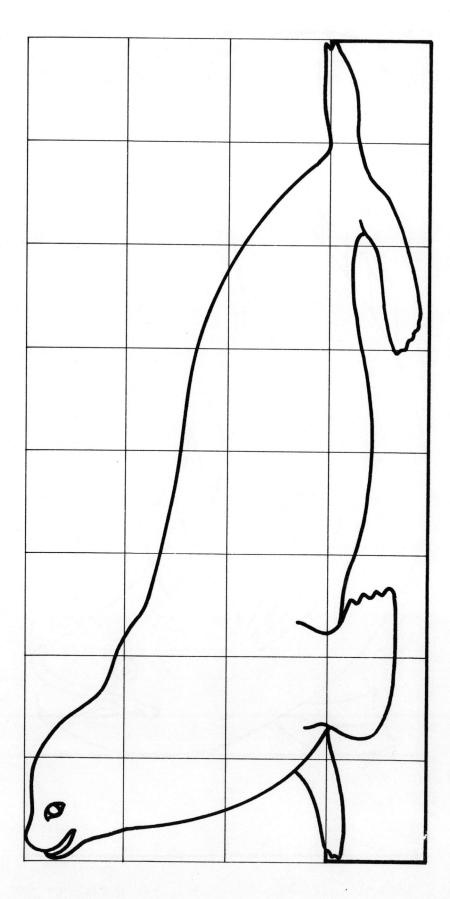

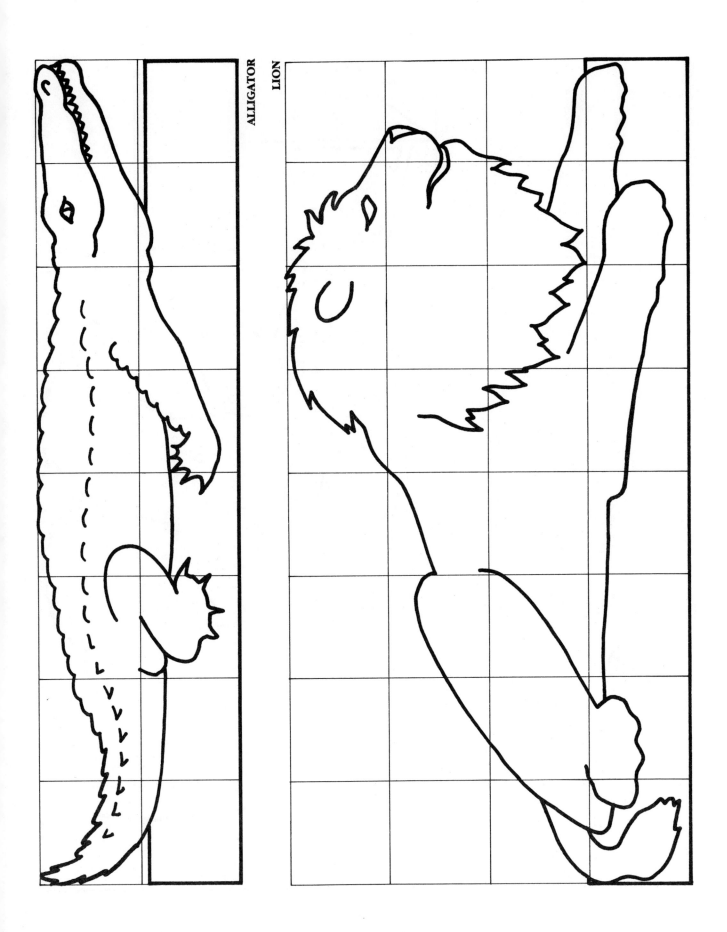

ALLIGATOR

LION

BEAR

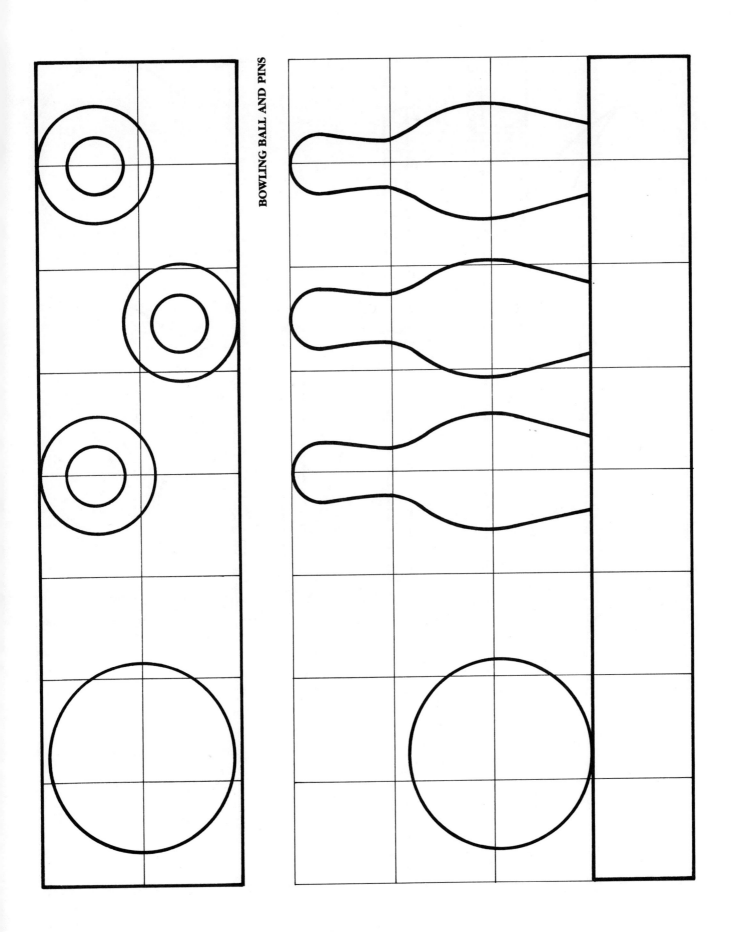

BOWLING BALL AND PINS

FOOTBALL AND HELMET

I LOVE N.Y. (or other initials)

(Courtesy of State of New York Dept. of Commerce)

PIANO

SLEIGH

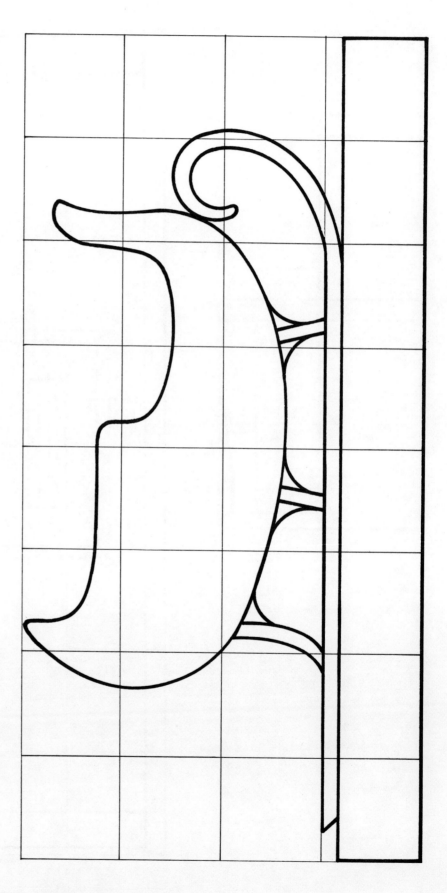

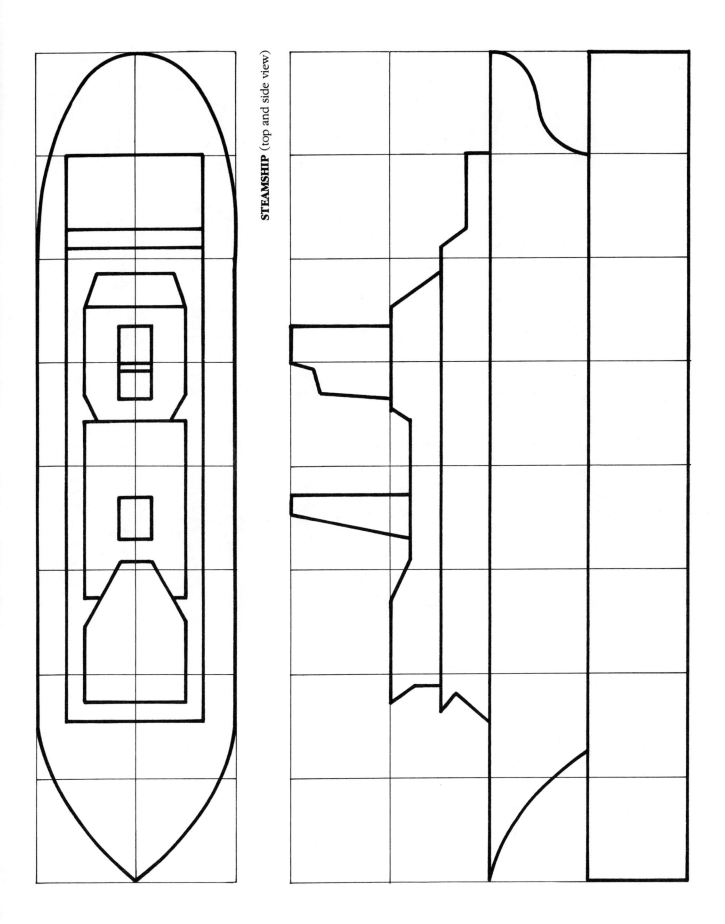

STEAMSHIP (top and side view)

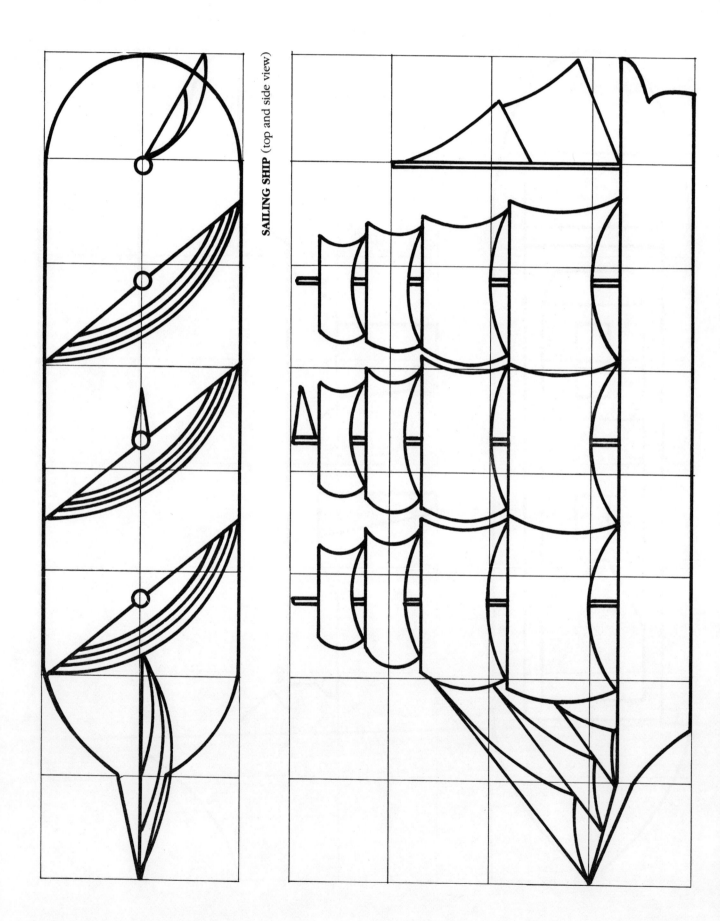

SAILING SHIP (top and side view)

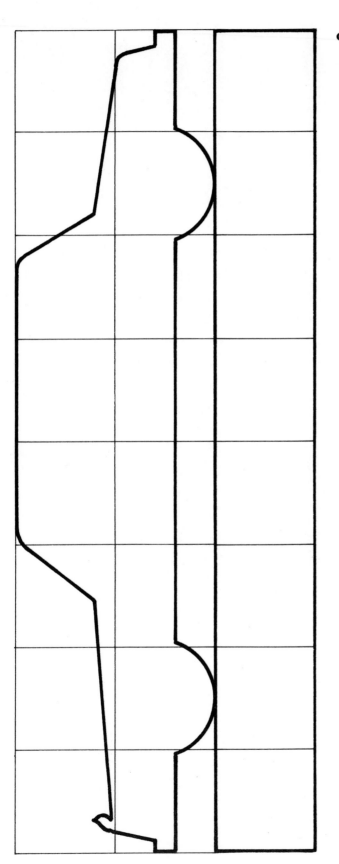

CAR